"By reading this book of J. D. Payne's, you ҆ ... ̶̶̶̶ .... opo...
tunities created by global migration and inspired by the real-life stories
and case studies of how seemingly ordinary folks can participate in the
Great Commission by implementing his proposed action plan—reaching
out to new neighbors in the West from abroad with the gospel, then partnering with them in kingdom efforts. This is a practical guide for Christians who embrace the vision of global mission and engage in local action."

Enoch Wan, president, Evangelical Missiological Society, and director,
Institute of Diaspora Studies, Western Seminary

"J. D. Payne has provided an excellent resource for the church in the West
to be involved with 'missions at its doorstep.' Scholarly yet written in a very
approachable style, full of interesting and illustrative stories, this book is a
wonderful addition to the small but growing literature on 'diaspora missiology.' It merits wide reading by academics, church leaders and lay
members of congregations alike."

Steven Ybarrola, professor of cultural anthropology,
Asbury Theological Seminary

"J. D. Payne is at it again with another perceptive and prophetic call to the
Great Commission community! With the perfect blend of Scripture,
stories and strategies, this book turns us toward our global diaspora future.
Read it with careful attention to what the sovereign God is doing in our
time—and with a commitment to be in step with his work in the world."

Grant McClung, president, Missions Resource Group

"With an eye toward Scripture, J. D. Payne has helpfully narrated the
history and present reality of 'peoples on the move.' Yet he takes the conversation one necessary step further and offers practical advice for Western
Christians to welcome the nations and effectively reach the ends of the
earth in their Jerusalem."

Edward Smither, professor of int[?]
Columbia International University

"The author summons an urgent invitation to Christians and the church in the West to live missionally *now*! Both the statistical information of the migration of global strangers and the biblical inspiration of the sovereign God's orchestration for kingdom expansion are convincing and compelling for us to seize the amazing harvest opportunities in our neighborhoods."

T. V. Thomas, chair, Ethnic America Network (EAN)

"It is shocking how negligent the Western church has been in reaching the peoples of the world that God has brought to us—especially compared to how active we have been in leaving our countries to go to them! *Strangers Next Door* clearly depicts the opportunity before us, and most excitingly, shares great stories of those already having a global impact by reaching the 'stranger next door.'"

Chris Clayman, church-planting catalyst with the North American Mission Board, team leader with Global Gates, and author of *ethNYcity: The Nations, Tongues, and Faiths of Metropolitan New York*

"*Strangers Next Door* is informative, insightful, inspirational and instructional to mission researchers and practitioners; clergy and parishioners; and missiology professors and students. J. D. Payne presents us with a great contribution to the fast-emerging diaspora missiology discourse. It summons the global church to action!"

Sadiri Joy Tira, senior associate for diasporas for The Lausanne Movement and vice president for diaspora missions with Advancing Indigenous Missions

"*Strangers Next Door* is a candid admission that a strategic frontier of world missions in the 21st century has returned to the home front. This book will charm readers with heart-rending anecdotes, relevant surveys and the author's insightful analysis of the realities in the changing landscape of missions within the borders of the Western world. This is perhaps J. D. Payne's most fascinating, coherent and convincing work on diaspora missiology to date!"

Tereso C. Casiño, professor of missiology and intercultural studies, School of Divinity, Gardner-Webb University, and executive chair, North America Diaspora Educators Forum (Global Diaspora Network)

"The world has not only shrunk; it has become energetic and mobile. It might be a tad clichéd to say it, but the world is now on our doorstep, which requires us to take the gospel seriously and devise a mission strategy to reach, train, partner and resource our global neighbors as they return to their homes with the gospel. J. D. Payne has presented us with the gospel imperative to take responsibility for those from all over the world who are among us. Some books impress you with their fresh insight, while others hit you with a clear and compelling statement of the obvious. This book does the latter, and it does it very well indeed."

Steve Timmis, Director for Acts 29 Western Europe

"A wide-eyed look at one of most strategic missiological opportunities for the church today. I was encouraged by Payne's presentation of the possibilities and convicted by our failure to thus far capitalize on them. What if the leaders for the completion of the Great Commission were right now 'visitors' in our cities?"

J. D. Greear, author of *Gospel: Recovering the Power That Made Christianity Revolutionary* and *Breaking the Islam Code*

"Many in our society—and even within our churches—see immigration as a threat or an invasion, but J. D. Payne challenges us to see immigration as Scripture does: as a missional opportunity. Many immigrants bring a vibrant faith with them to their new country, breathing new life into local churches, but others do not yet know the hope of a transformational relationship with Jesus. If we have the eyes to see it, immigration presents an opportunity to 'make disciples of all nations' without even leaving our zip codes, and *Strangers Next Door* serves as an informative and practical guide."

Matthew Soerens, U.S. church training specialist at World Relief and coauthor of *Welcoming the Stranger: Justice, Compassion & Truth in the Immigration Debate*

J. D. Payne

Strangers
Next Door

Immigration,
Migration and Mission

IVP Books

An imprint of InterVarsity Press
Downers Grove, Illinois

InterVarsity Press
P.O. Box 1400, Downers Grove, IL 60515-1426
World Wide Web: www.ivpress.com
E-mail: email@ivpress.com

InterVarsity Press® is the book-publishing division of InterVarsity Christian Fellowship/USA®, a movement of students and faculty active on campus at hundreds of universities, colleges and schools of nursing in the United States of America, and a member movement of the International Fellowship of Evangelical Students. For information about local and regional activities, write Public Relations Dept., InterVarsity Christian Fellowship/USA, 6400 Schroeder Rd., P.O. Box 7895, Madison, WI 53707-7895, or visit the IVCF website at <www.intervarsity.org>.

While all stories in this book are true, some names and identifying information in this book have been changed to protect the privacy of the individuals involved.

Excerpts from Who Is My Neighbor? Reaching Internationals in North America by Phillip and Kandace Connor (Princeton, NJ: n.p., 2008) is used by permission. Available from www.reachinternationals.com.

ISBN 978-0-8308-5758-6

Printed in the United States of America ∞

Library of Congress Cataloging-in-Publication Data has been requested.

P	18	17	16	15	14	13	12	11	10	9	8	7	6	5	4	3	2	1
Y	27	26	25	24	23	22	21	20	19	18	17	16	15	14	13	12			

To my heavenly Father,
who oversees the movements of the nations,

and to Sarah,
whom he moved into my life

■ ■ ■

OTHER BOOKS BY J. D. PAYNE

Missional House Churches:
Reaching Our Communities with the Gospel

The Barnabas Factors:
Eight Essential Practices of Church Planting Team Members

Discovering Church Planting:
An Introduction to the Whats, Whys, and Hows
of Global Church Planting

Evangelism:
A Biblical Response to Today's Questions

Contents

Acknowledgments

I AM THANKFUL THAT YOU HAVE DECIDED to read this book. While my name is on the cover, you would not be reading these words without the assistance of some great people, and in this section I wish to thank them. Of course, I take full responsibility for any limitations or errors in this work.

Thank you, Renee Emerson, for your administrative assistance and the development of many of the tables contained in this book. I must also thank my research assistant, Matt Pierce, for his labors of tracking down numerous resources for me.

Thank you, Volney James and the several individuals making up your committee. I appreciate your heart for the nations and for believing in this project. Thank you to my editor, John Dunham, and your team for your labors. And thank you, Mike Dworak and Dean Galiano, for all that you guys do to help spread the word about this book. Shortly after writing this book for Biblica Books, this division of Biblica Worldwide was acquired by InterVarsity Press. It has been a tremendous blessing working with the people of IVP. They have greatly assisted with this work and are to be commended for their professionalism and encouraging spirit. I truly appreciate all that you have done on this project.

Of course, I must say thank you to Sarah, the greatest wife and mother in the world! And also, thanks to Hannah, Rachel, and Joel as well. I truly appreciate all of your prayers and sacrifices to make this book a reality.

Most of all, I must offer a word of thanksgiving to the Lord. It has been a blessing to work on this book. His grace to me is amazing.

Introduction

SAMUEL AND YOUNG CHO ARE A MIDDLE-AGED Korean couple living in Lutherville, Maryland.[1] Korean is their heart language and English is their second language. A few years ago, the Lord used this couple to begin Nepal Church of Baltimore, after they met a Nepalese waitress and her family. Recently, the Chos also planted a Bhutani church in Baltimore.

The Nepalese, whether from Nepal or Bhutan, are considered among the world's least reached peoples . . . and they live in Baltimore, Maryland, USA.

In 2008 the Chos took a short-term mission trip to Nepal and visited the families of the church members living in Baltimore. In Nepal, one family invited other family members to hear Samuel preach. Several people came to faith and the Antioch Church in Jamsa was planted. By the conclusion of the trip, over two hundred people had made a profession of faith in Jesus.

Did I mention the Nepalese are considered among the world's least reached peoples . . . and they live in Baltimore, Maryland, USA?

Shortly after returning from their first missionary trip, the Chos decided to take a second trip to Nepal to minister to refugees and also to travel into India. After finally arriving in a Jhapa refugee camp in southeast Nepal, the Chos were able to locate relatives of members of the Nepal Church of Baltimore. During this visit the Chos were able to share letters and gifts from family members in the States. One of the family members living in Nepal made a profession of faith in Jesus.

While on this second missionary trip, the Chos were able to plant two more churches and to observe two hundred Nepalese, three hundred Bhutanese, and thirty-five Indians make professions of faith in Jesus.

And it began when Koreans in living in Maryland started evangelizing and planting churches with Nepalese living in their neighborhood.

What if more believers like the Chos took seriously the need to cross cultural barriers and take the gospel to the least reached peoples living in the Western world, where the challenges to getting the gospel to the people are not as daunting as trying to reach them in their homelands? What if more kingdom citizens living in Western nations recognized the Great Commission opportunity set before them—that the Sovereign Lord has moved the world into their neighborhoods so that such peoples may become his followers?

Imagine the global possibilities if churches would serve, share the good news, plant churches, partner with, and send the least reached peoples of the world back to their families, tribes, villages, and cities as missionaries. Believers living in the West have dreamed and talked about these possibilities for some time. While some churches have moved beyond talking and are doing it, far too many kingdom citizens remain oblivious to the needs in their neighborhoods and the Great Commission potential that exists.

While the perspective used in this book is unique and contemporary, the notion of reaching those who migrate to our countries and sending them home with the good news is not new. For example, Frank Obien, in his book *Building Bridges of Love: A Handbook for Sharing God's Love with International Students*, wrote that in the 1960s he noticed that while missionaries were traveling the world, international students were coming to the United States—only to return without anyone sharing the gospel with them.[2] Don Bjork, in a 1985 *Christianity Today* article, attempted to raise awareness of the migration of the nations to the United States. Commenting on the realities in the 1970s and 1980s, he wrote:

Millions of strange new faces began appearing on the streets of American cities, collectively changing the face of the nation itself. But who in the church really noticed? Unseen or unheeded, the fields at home were long since "white unto harvest." Yet right down to the end of the 1970s, few missions leaders really knew what was going on. The "invisible migrants" took no pains to hide, yet it seemed few missions took pains to seek.[3]

Progress has been made since Bjork's article, but unfortunately it is too little and too slow. While such discussions have taken place in the past, most evangelicals have been slow to respond. The good news is that more and more people, churches, networks, denominations, societies, and mission agencies are talking about this topic once again and starting to act on the need.

Many of the world's least reached peoples live in our communities. Now is the time to cross the street and meet the strangers next door.

THE BEGINNING OF THIS BOOK

Authors always have reasons for writing books. For some time I had been thinking and lecturing on the topic of migration and the Great Commission but never felt strongly compelled to write a book on the topic. I knew such a work needed to be produced, but the vision for this book did not become a reality until one day during a conversation with my mother.

One afternoon we were talking about the Appalachian region of the United States. In particular, we were discussing a community in Laurel County, Kentucky, known as Swiss Colony, just a few miles north of my hometown. My mother noted that the name of that community quite possibly came from the migration of the Swiss into the southeastern part of the state, bringing their dairy skills, culture, and their faith traditions. I knew many European peoples migrated into Virginia, Kentucky, and Tennessee through places like Cumberland

Gap in southeastern Kentucky. The thought of such people settling in Laurel County was not a surprise to me. However, the more I thought about the origins of Swiss Colony—an area far from Switzerland both geographically and culturally—the more the Lord started to stir my thoughts regarding global evangelization and migration and the opportunities for the church in the Western nations of the world.

The more I prayed and researched the topic of migration to Western countries, the more I realized how the church was missing out on a significant opportunity to reach, model, equip, partner, and send many people groups back to their peoples across the globe. For centuries the church has been sending missionaries to the least reached peoples across the globe. While this practice *must* continue, we also must recognize that over the years large numbers of peoples have been migrating to Western nations, peoples that have been categorized by missiologists as the world's least reached people groups (or unreached people groups).

THE PURPOSE OF THIS BOOK

Such global movements of peoples across history, whether forced or voluntary, are under the eye of the Sovereign Lord. Migration does not occur by happenstance. This book is written from the conviction that God permits the movement of peoples across the globe in order to advance his kingdom. Some people move to locations that enable them to hear the good news (Acts 17:26–27). Others, who are kingdom citizens, move and are able to share the good news in their new locations (Acts 1:8). With these points in mind, the purpose of this book is twofold.

First, it is my desire to educate the Western church on the scope of global migrations that are taking place as the peoples of the world move to the West in search of a better way of life. At present there are large numbers of believers and unbelievers migrating to Western nations. Much of the Western church is fairly ignorant as to the numbers, cultures, and beliefs of such peoples.

Second, I want to challenge the Western church to reach the least reached people living in their neighborhoods and partner with them to return to their peoples as missionaries. An enormous Great Commission opportunity exists that seems to be going unnoticed by the church. The United States, Canada, the United Kingdom, other Western European nations, Australia, and New Zealand presently receive an enormous portion of the world's migrants, with the United States receiving the largest percentage of those migrating to the Western world. Refugees, students, long-term and temporary workers, and immigrants move to these regions of the world every year.

At the time of this writing, the opportunities for ministering to such peoples are as simple as locating them, finding out their needs, and serving them with the love of Jesus. Obtaining visas is not a problem. Overcoming governmental opposition to missionary activity is not an issue. Western churches can easily begin welcoming and serving the strangers next door with little preparation. As migrants come to faith in Jesus, there are numerous opportunities for equipping, partnering, commissioning, and sending those believers as missionaries back to their people to multiply disciples, leaders, and churches.

WHAT YOU WILL NOT FIND HERE

I remember being in a restaurant and ordering a dish that sounded good, based on the menu's description. I was greatly surprised when the meal arrived. What I thought was going to be a delightful chicken dish covered with a mild sauce turned out to be a plate filled with chicken smothered in liquid fire! My expectations did not meet reality. And several gallons of water later, I remained greatly disappointed.

As you read this book, I do not want you to expect one thing and then receive something disappointing. Therefore it is important that I state from the outset what this book is *not* about. While I believe that the following matters are extremely important and that the church must speak to these issues, it is not my desire to address them in this book.

First, this book is not about the political issues revolving around immigration and refugees. As I write this introduction, countries such as France and the United States are facing numerous political debates on the topic of immigration. Second, this work will spend little, if any, space addressing the ethical issues regarding immigration and how people should respond. While there are chapters addressing what the Scriptures advocate regarding migration, I will not attempt to offer a practical response to the moral and ethical dilemma concerning how the church should address undocumented immigrants and immigrant quotas. Third, this book does not address how a church should respond to the cultural shifts that occur whenever its membership significantly increases in the number of minority peoples, sometimes resulting in local church conflicts. Fourth, while this book recognizes that the Majority World churches are now sending missionaries to Western countries and that the future dominant missionary force is likely to come primarily from the non-Western world, this book will not address the changing demographic and cultural shape of the Christian faith. For such information I will direct you to works such as Philip Jenkins's *The Next Christendom: The Coming of Global Christianity*.[4]

This book is not written to an exclusively North American audience. While I must state my American bias from the outset and admit that more attention is devoted to what is happening in my neighborhood, it has been my desire to write for a wider Western audience, at least by noting migration matters related to other Western countries. I want to help you catch a vision for your neighborhood. Because I wish to leave you with an impression rather than a comprehensive look at the West, this book does not provide a detailed treatment for every Western country. And since I am the most familiar with migration issues in the United States, I beg for some grace whenever my ignorance is revealed regarding other Western nations.

I also am aware that what constitutes *the West* or *Western coun-tries* varies from group to group. For the purposes of this book, whenever I use these terms, I am referring to the United States, Canada, Australia, New Zealand, and many of the countries commonly referred to as Western Europe. While I am aware that many of the countries of this latter region are technically from Northern and Southern Europe, I have placed them all together for a few reasons. First, for some time *Western* has been closely linked to industrialized nations with a certain general Judeo-Christian worldview that is distinctive from Eastern countries. Also, the West has been understood as a collection of nations that are separate from the Majority World, thus maintaining several common cultural distinctions. Finally, the Western countries have also been places of great evangelical growth, with little religious persecution or threat to missionaries and churches.

Even in light of the fact that the United States receives the overwhelming majority of the annual migrants to the Western world, very large numbers of people are arriving in Western Europe, Australia, and New Zealand. While I recognize there are geographical, cultural, and political differences among kingdom citizens living in Western nations, we are all part of the same body of Christ. And the Great Commission applies to us all. Regardless of our location, as kingdom citizens we are to carry the never-changing gospel to an ever-changing world. As kingdom citizens living in Western nations, we have enormous freedoms and opportunities to reach some of the least reached people with the good news. This book is a call for Western Christians to live missional lives in their neighborhoods as they labor for the day when heaven proclaims, "The kingdom of the world has become the kingdom of our Lord and of his Christ, and he shall reign forever and ever" (Revelation 11:15).

THE DIVINE MAESTRO

From a human perspective, the global movement of people from one geographical location to another is sometimes chalked up to sociocultural *push-pull* realities. War and famine push people out of East Africa while the promise of safety and a better life pulls them to France. A poor educational system in India pushes students out of their homeland to follow the pull of a better education in the United States. This view of the migration of peoples across the globe is a complex matter of economics, power, freedom, justice, and a better way of life. While such social forces are at work in our world today, we must realize that through such means the Sovereign Lord is working to bring about the expansion of his kingdom. Since the world is presently under the rule of the gods of this age, human wickedness sometimes brings slavery, hardships, death, and destruction, resulting in the forced migration of peoples. Yet the God of the ages is still in control while all of creation groans for his return (Romans 8:22).

The premise of this book is that the Sovereign Lord orchestrates the movement of peoples across the globe in order to advance his kingdom for his glory. Whether through believers transferring jobs and finding themselves in new locations or unbelievers moving to cities of refuge where they may first come face-to-face with the message of Jesus, the migrations of peoples do not happen as an afterthought in the heart of God. The church may be oblivious to such workings of the Spirit, but the seasons and times of life are part of the King working out his plan to redeem the peoples of this world from the bondage of the wicked one.

Until that day when the kingdoms of this world will all bow to the true King, the church is to be on a mission, making disciples of all nations and teaching them obedience (Matthew 28:20). While a major part of making disciples occurs as we go throughout the world (Matthew 28:19), we must realize that the divine Maestro has been orchestrating the movement of peoples into our neighborhoods. He has been bringing the peoples of the uttermost parts of the world into our communities. While this book *in no way* diminishes the importance of churches in the Western world going to other nations to reach peoples with the gospel, this book does offer a challenge to Western churches: what are you doing to reach, equip, partner with, and send the strangers next door back to their loved ones with the good news? Are they simply strangers with strange ways, or do you realize the Great Commission opportunity that is present?

OTHER WRITINGS TO DATE

At the time I am writing, this book is one of only a few resources that attempt to address the issue of migration to Western nations in light of the Great Commission. I certainly hope this situation changes soon, for the need is great for such publications. Thorsten Prill's *Global Mission on Our Doorstep: Forced Migration and the Future of the Church* is a helpful work related to understanding the realities for mission that migration provides. Philip and Kandace Connor self-published *Who Is My Neighbor? Reaching Internationals in North America*, a small but excellent book on the topic. Glenn Rogers has written *North American Cross-Cultural Church Planting*, addressing the need for cross-cultural work and methods for planting churches among immigrants. Other recent publications that have been helpful include David Boyd's *You Don't Have to Cross the Ocean to Reach the World: The Power of Local Cross-Cultural Ministry* and Donna S. Thomas's *Faces in the Crowd: Reaching Your International Neighbor for Christ.*

Several years ago Tom Phillips and Bob Norsworthy wrote *The World at Your Door: Reaching International Students in Your Home, Church, and School;* Lawson Lau wrote *The World at Your Doorstep: A Handbook for International Student Ministry;* and Brian Seim edited *Canada's New Harvest: Helping Churches Touch Newcomers.*

There is a growing new category in the area of missions known as *diaspora missiology*, which I will briefly discuss in a later chapter.

There is a small but growing amount of literature in this area. Enoch
Wan edited *Missions Within Reach: Intercultural Ministries in Canada*,
coedited with Sadiri Joy Tira *Missions Practice in the 21ˢᵗ Century*, and
coedited with Michael Pocock *Missions from the Majority World:
Progress, Challenges, and Case Studies*. These three works contain a
wealth of chapters related to reaching, equipping, and sending migrants across the world. Luis Pantoja Jr., Sadiri Joy Tira, and Enoch
Wan edited *Scattered: The Filipino Global Presence*, which examines
the work of believers comprising the Filipino diaspora. Jehu J. Hanciles examined the African diaspora in his recent work *Beyond Christendom: Globalization, African Migration, and the Transformation of
the West*. And S. Hun Kim and Wonsuk Ma edited a book on the
Korean diaspora titled *Korean Diaspora and Christian Mission*.

While this book draws from many of these excellent publications, it
offers the first extensive treatment of the connection of missions and
migration to the West. While this book is a serious scholarly treatment of
the topic including much statistical data, I have worked hard to prevent
it from reading like an academic treatise. My desire from the beginning
has been that you will be able to grasp the truth of a very weighty issue
and make practical adjustments in life and ministry in relation to the
Great Commission opportunities that migration provides.

So now that you have a glimpse of what this book addresses, I
invite you to travel with me into the world of global migrations. As
you read through this book, it is my prayer that you will develop a
vision for the harvest fields that will result in action. I hope that you
will develop a heart for reaching, equipping, partnering, and sending
migrants to the least reached nations of the world. The Lord of the
harvest is actively at work in his world through the movement of
peoples for the advancement of his kingdom. May the strangers next
door that you meet this morning become your brothers and sisters in
the Lord this afternoon and go to the nations later this evening.

Immigration, Migration, and Kingdom Perspective

My name is Jo. I left my country six years ago looking for hope and a better life for my family. I came to this country to find a higher paying job so that I could take care of my wife and five children. I came here so my children could have an opportunity to receive a good education. I moved to here in search of prosperity. What I found was twelve-hour workdays and very little time with my children. The longer we are here, the more I fear my children will forget who they are and where they come from; I want them to remember our language, our culture, and our family values. Very few people have befriended us. I miss the tight-knit community in my home country. We are so lonely here. Where is our hope? Who will be our friend?

■　　■　　■

My name is Fatima. I came to this country five years ago with my eleven children after my husband was killed during the war in my country. Before coming to this country, we spent many years in a refugee camp in another country near our home. Life there was very hard. We had little food, and there was no schooling for my children. I gave birth to my youngest child in that camp. Then we received the news that we were allowed to come to this country. We did not know the language and had very little money. When we arrived in the city, we lived in a bad part of town. I was mugged once and my children were harassed daily. We were completely lost and lonely. My knowledge of the language *is still poor. We all still have nightmares about the things that happened in our own country. We also fear what will happen to us here in this new country. How will we survive? Does anyone care?*

■   ■   ■

My name is May. I am an international student at the university. My dream is to become very successful and make my family and my country proud. It is a great honor to be able to come to this country to study, but taking classes in a different language is very hard. It is also difficult to be separated from my family. In my country, three generations of a family usually live together in one house. Here at the university, I live all by myself. I spend a great amount of time studying, and most of the time I am lonely. I want to get to know some nationals, but everyone seems so busy and like they are in such a hurry. Does anyone care? Who will be my family while I am here?[1]

■   ■   ■

While not all migrants share the same stories, Jo, Fatima, and May represent a great number of people migrating to countries across the world. For some, migration offers hope for a better way of life financially and educationally; for others, migration provides a way to escape persecution, war, and death. Highly skilled specialists and entrepreneurs migrate to a much better standard of living and quality of life than the family that is forced to relocate because of genocide. Some individuals and families move to other countries to be greeted by family and friends who preceded them, and who are able to offer some stability and security to their newly arriving relatives. Others arrive as students, refugees, or workers, knowing few, if any, people.

Though the stories are not exactly alike, all migrants have stories to tell. While it is important for us to hear such stories, having a kingdom perspective requires that we are praying and looking for opportunities for the stories of migrants to intersect with the story of Jesus, so that their future stories involve him.

TERMINOLOGY AND TYPES OF MIGRATION

At the risk of being labeled too simplistic when it comes to the topic of migration, I offer some simple explanations and definitions of commonly used words in the field of migration studies. Since this is not a book primarily addressing migration theories or contemporary secular issues in migration studies, I will leave the more robust discussions and definitions to the work of other scholars. With such a disclaimer in mind, I want to turn your attention to a brief overview of the different types of migration.

In his work *The History of Human Migration*, Russell King shared three common divisions related to migration that will assist us in "creating a conceptual map of human mobility."[2] While King rightly recognized that there are limitations to these divisions (e.g., some migration situations cannot be easily divided but can be classified according to both divisions), migration is sometimes referred to as being *internal* or *international* (e.g., moving to a different location in one's country versus moving to a different country altogether); *forced* or *voluntary* (e.g., moving due to being forced into slavery versus moving out of a desire to live with relatives); and *permanent* or *temporary* (e.g., moving for indefinite employment versus moving for seasonal employment).[3]

While these three common divisions are helpful to keep in mind, it is also important that you are aware of the meanings of a few words used throughout this book. *Migration* is the movement of a people from one location of residence to another location of residence. Throughout this book, I use this term to refer to a very broad range of people on the move. *Migrants* can refer to those who would be categorized as long-term workers or short-term workers, students, refugees, stateless peoples, asylum seekers, and people in the process of immigrating as well as those who have immigrated to another country.

Immigration is understood as the movement of a people into a different country to settle.

Emigration is the departure from one's country to settle elsewhere.

Refugee can be a challenging word to define, so I will use a commonly accepted definition. According to the United Nations Refugee Agency, the 1951 Refugee Convention establishing the United Nations High Commissioner for Refugees notes that a *refugee* is a person "owing to a well-founded fear of being persecuted for reasons of race, religion, nationality, membership of a particular social group or political opinion, is outside the country of his nationality, and is unable to, or owing to such fear, is unwilling to avail himself of the protection of that country."[4] An *asylum seeker* is a person who claims to be a refugee, but whose claim has not yet been definitively evaluated.[5]

I recognize that we typically hear the word *immigration* used more often than *migration*. It should be noted, however, that throughout this book I often use the latter word to communicate the overarching notion of the movement of all kinds of peoples across the world. While issues related to the movement of peoples from one country to another to settle for permanent residence (immigration) are very important matters today, the church must recognize that such movements are not limited only to those who will take up citizenship in another land but include the temporary resident as well.

Stephen Castles and Mark J. Miller offered some helpful information regarding two additionally important terms: *foreign born* and *foreign national*:

The foreign born include persons who have become *naturalized*, that is, who have taken on the nationality (or citizenship) of the receiving country. . . . The category excludes children born to immigrants in the receiving country (the *second generation*) if they are citizens of that country. The term *foreign nationals* excludes those who have taken on the nationality of the receiving country, but includes children born to immigrants who retain their parents' nationality (which can be a large proportion of the second and even third generations in countries which do not confer citizenship by right of birth).[6]

KINGDOM PERSPECTIVE ON GLOBAL MIGRATIONS

The history of humanity is a history of migration. Ever since the exodus from Eden (Genesis 3:23–24), men and women have been on the move. The expansion of the Europeans in the 1500s began a new era in the history of migration. While the nineteenth and twentieth centuries recorded large movements of peoples across the globe, mainly from Europe to the United States, the latter part of the twentieth and early twenty-first century has revealed that migration is now more of a global phenomenon. Globalization—with advances in telecommunications, faster and safer forms of transportation, as well as new political structures—has helped facilitate the movement of large numbers of people on a global scale. Such matters have caught the attention of many scholars. Castles and Miller titled their highly praised book *The Age of Migration* because numerous momentous events across the globe now involve international migration. And according to these authors, there are several reasons to expect this age of migration to continue:

Growing inequalities in wealth between the North and South are likely to impel increasing numbers of people to move in search of better living standards; political, environmental, and

demographic pressures may force many people to seek refuge
outside their own countries; political or ethnic conflict in a
number of regions could lead to future mass flights; and the
creation of new free trade areas will cause movements of labor,
whether or not this is intended by the governments concerned.
But migration is not just a reaction to difficult conditions at
home; it is also motivated by the search for better opportunities and lifestyles elsewhere. It is not just the poor who move;
movements between rich countries are increasing too. Economic development of poorer countries can actually lead to
greater migration because it gives people the resources to move.
Some migrants experience abuse or exploitation, but most
benefit and are able to improve their lives through mobility.
Conditions may be tough for migrants but are often preferable
to poverty, insecurity, and lack of opportunities at home—
otherwise migration would not continue.[7]

While the sociological and anthropological discussions for the migrations of people explain such movements in humanistic categories
(e.g., war, persecution, education, economics), as kingdom citizens
we understand that the Lord of the nations is working out his will in
the universe, and the migration of peoples to other lands is not a
serendipitous occurrence. Such is particularly true with the migration of the world's least reached people groups to areas of the
world where they can freely encounter the gospel of Jesus Christ.

THE THEOLOGICAL ASSUMPTION

Even a cursory reading of the Scriptures reveals that the God who
created the heavens and earth is very much engaged with his creation.
He is both transcendent and imminent. He is not the god of deism,
who created the world and then wandered off to some distant corner
of the universe to let it all wind down on its own like some cosmo-

logical clock. He is not the impotent god of the process theologians, always hanging on to the edge of his seat, wondering what will happen next in the universe and freaking out because things are out of his control. Rather, the Scriptures portray an omnipotent and omniscient God who is sovereign over everything. While his creation may not necessarily understand his thoughts and ways (Isaiah 55:8–9), he is working out everything for the good of his people and his glory.

So how do these characteristics of God connect with global migrations of millions of people? Simply, God is at work in the world, in the good times and the bad times. He is at work through the mass movements of peoples from the rural communities to the cities, from persecution, war, and starvation to lands of security and prosperity, and from areas where educational and economic lift are rare to locations where such matters are assumed to be the norm.

In his address on Mars Hill, the apostle Paul spoke to the polytheistic Athenians about this God. His presentation included an important reference noting that the Lord is sovereign over his creation, specifically over history and people. Luke recorded, "And he made from one man every nation of mankind to live on all the face of the earth, having determined allotted periods and the boundaries of their dwelling place, that they should seek God, and perhaps feel their way toward him and find him. Yet he is actually not far from each one of us" (Acts 17:26–27).

While this is a significant passage in Paul's Mars Hill address, these two verses are not the easiest to understand from the original Greek language in which they were written. Though scholars have argued over the exact meaning of the words, the point of the passage is to show that the God whom Paul proclaims is the Sovereign Lord over his creation and that people should come to him.[8] While the peoples of the world are scattered across the earth, they all share a common father and mother, Adam and Eve, and a common Creator.

Paul also noted that the God he proclaimed is the Sovereign Lord over history. While the peoples of the world have migrated across the earth since the first family departed from Eden, the Lord has been in control of the times of their lives and locations of residence. His divine hand has been working through such global migrations so that humans in their depraved state may come to know the grace of the imminent Creator.

While the next two chapters of this book offer a biblical perspective on global migrations, it is important to note here that the rise and fall of nations and the movements of peoples across the globe are a part of the outworking of the Lord's plan leading to the day when his kingdom will come (Matthew 6:10) and all the nations will bow and worship him (Psalm 86:9; Isaiah 2:2; Philippians 2:9–11). He is the God who rules over the nations (Daniel 4; 2 Chronicles 20:6; Psalm 22:28) and is presently working through his church to preach the good news to the peoples of this world before the end comes (Matthew 24:14; Mark 13:10). While the Lord does not cause evil, he does work through the wickedness of others to accomplish this plan, such as the scattering of Israel among the nations (Deuteronomy 30:1) and the scattering of the Jerusalem church at the hand of persecution (Acts 11:19–20). From the migration out of Eden (Genesis 2:23–24), the Lord has been working out his salvation history as people have multiplied and spread across the planet (Genesis 9:1, 7; 35:11).

THE MISSIOLOGICAL ASSUMPTION

If the Lord of history and creation is actively engaged in his creation (Psalm 139; John 1:14; Galatians 4:4) so that people may come to follow him, then he has provided a means whereby the peoples of this world will come to experience his salvation and abundant life (John 10:10). This divine means is the proclamation of the gospel by his church (Romans 1:16; 10:14–15). Since he has commanded his followers to make disciples of all nations (Matthew 28:19), the expectation is that his church will walk in obedience to this Great Commission.

While we must continue to send missionaries throughout the world, we must also recognize the Great Commission opportunity that is present in Western nations. Something is missiologically malignant when we are willing to send people across the oceans, risking life and limb and spending enormous amounts of money, but we are not willing to walk next door and minister to the strangers living there. Again, we must continue to go to the nations, but we must also remember that the nations have come to us.

The Lord of the harvest has been moving some of the world's unreached and least reached peoples to countries where governmental opposition will not interfere with missionary labors and where obtaining a visa and the costs of travel are not issues. The church in the West must remember her missional nature and function intentionally, strategically, and apostolically.

It is not enough to know that least reached peoples are living in our communities; rather, we must be intentional about ministering to them. The wise steward recognizes that the Lord has provided these opportunities for us for such a time as this. It is necessary that we begin to think strategically. How can we reach these people with the news of the gospel? How can we model before them a simple, yet biblical, understanding of church life that would be highly reproducible by them among their people groups across the world? How can we equip them and partner with them as they are sent as missionaries to their families, friends, and others throughout their social networks? These are just a few questions that the church in the West must be asking in light of global migrations. Such questions, along with others, will be addressed throughout this book to help us think about the Great Commission opportunities in our contexts.

Now that you have a general idea of the kingdom perspective behind my understanding of global migrations, it is time to ask the question, What in the world is God doing? In order to answer to this question, let's turn to chapter 2.

What in the World Is God Doing?

PEOPLES ON THE MOVE

The largest nationalities granted British citizenship in 2010 were Indian (29,405), Pakistani (22,054), Filipino (9,429), Bangladeshi (7,966), and Chinese (7,581).[1]

The proportion of babies born to mothers from outside the UK recently reached a record high of 24.7%. Newham, in east London, is the area with the highest proportion of such births—more than 75%—with Pakistan, Poland, and India topping the list for the mothers' countries of origin.[2]

■   ■   ■

For centuries Western nations have been receiving non-Western migrants. So, in one sense, the West has been influenced by the East for some time. However, by the beginning of the twenty-first century, things had changed. Globalization has caused the world to shrink, and now mobility has become easier and affects all regions of the world. Instead of taking months to journey to another country, we can now make the trip in a matter of hours. What was once considered foreign is now commonplace.

While it is possible to debate the influence of the West on the rest of the world, a simple examination of the statistical data of global migrations reveals that a large number of people, whether forced or not, continue to locate in Western countries each year. Many of these peoples migrate from non-Western, Majority World nations. On closer examination, we begin to realize that many of these strangers next door actually represent some of the world's unreached and least reached people groups. While we rightly call out, equip, and send brothers and sisters to the nations to preach the gospel, many times we are unaware that our neighbors across the street or down the hall are of the very people group to whom we send missionaries.

ARE MR. SINGH AND AUNTIE THE STRANGERS NEXT DOOR TO YOU?

While living in Montreal, Canada, Phillip and Kandace Connor were able to develop a relationship with Mr. Singh and Auntie, a Punjabi couple. The following is their story:

> We were about to knock on their door when it suddenly opened for us, releasing a strong aroma of curry into the hallway. There was Mr. Singh. A man of about 45 years, Mr. Singh looked like he was really in his late fifties. He had a rugged appearance with an uneven, graying beard, rough leather skin, and large wrinkles under his eyes. He wore a simple baseball cap he probably picked up somewhere along the way at a thrift store. "Hello," was all he said with a smile, and we extended our arms to shake his hand. From behind the door peeked Mr. Singh's wife. She put her hand on her chest and said, "Auntie," and we responded with the same gesture stating our names. She was wearing a bright green and yellow shalwar kameez (a women's Indian dress) with matching green and yellow bangles on her arms. She just glanced at Phillip and directly went to Kandace with arms open wide, speaking all the while in Punjabi. She embraced Kandace, looked her straight in the face and said more words in Punjabi with a huge smile, laughing with glee. After a brief exchange between Mr. Singh

and Auntie in Punjabi, Mr. Singh asked, "You speak Punjabi?"
We shook our heads no. . . .

After Mr. Singh motioned to us to take a seat on the sofa,
he and Auntie sat down on the chairs beside us. Mr. Singh
went over to the television and picked up a video tape with a
picture of Jesus on the front, "You gave this?" he asked. We
shook our heads and said yes. "It's Punjabi," responded Mr.
Singh. We again shook our heads in agreement.

I (Phillip) finally got up the nerve to say something. "Did
you like it?"

"Ah, yes, I like it," replied Mr. Singh. . . .

As Mr. Singh and I sat watching, trying to discuss the film,
I heard a door creak. A younger man, clean shaven with a towel
in his hand, walked in from around the corner. I shook his
hand and introduced myself. Mr. Singh said something to him
in Punjabi, pointing at the television playing the Jesus film.
The younger man said, "You sent this to him. How did you get
it? Do you speak Punjabi?" As he hung his towel over the head-
board of the nearby bed, I explained that I did not speak
Punjabi but had friends who translated the film from English
into many different languages. It was becoming clear that this
younger man was a roommate of Mr. Singh and Auntie. He
shook my hand again and indicated he was going out for the
evening. Upon his departure, Mr. Singh took the telephone
and started calling many people, speaking all the while in
Punjabi. Once he finished his phone calls, he said, "Friends are
coming." Within fifteen minutes, two families arrived on the
scene. Women and children went into the kitchen with
Kandace and Auntie, while the men stayed in the living room.
The men's English was better than Mr. Singh's but still limited.
During the next hour, two more families arrived. The film
continued to play throughout, and everyone asked the same

basic questions, "Do you speak Punjabi? Where did you get this?" Between discussions about our work, our families, and where we were from, we all watched the film. That evening was a chaotic format for the proclamation of the gospel; but between the chicken curry and the cries of bored children, I had the opportunity to explain a few of the key parables Jesus told in the film. The gospel, at least in pieces, was proclaimed and it appeared this would not be our final opportunity to meet with Mr. Singh and his friends. . . .

After a few months, Mr. Singh asked us if we had any extra films we could send to his village in India. It was not a problem to find funds for such a strategic task of proclamation. Mr. Singh gave us ten Indian addresses and we sent them out, not entirely confident they would ever reach their destination, given the simplicity of their addresses. Within a few weeks, Mr. Singh said they were all received and everyone enjoyed watching them. Only God knows the impact such a connection to India made on those who watched the Jesus film in Mr. Singh's village.[3]

The Lord of the harvest has been bringing the Mr. Singhs and Aunties of the world to Westerns nations. Where are they living in your communities? Do you fear trying to connect with them, not knowing their language? Does the smell of their foods keep you from befriending them? Does the potential for having such a chaotic relationship keep you away? Do you see the potential for kingdom advancement as you communicate the good news to the Mr. Singhs and Aunties, not just the potential for the transformation of lives in our communities but the transformation of lives in the villages of the Indias of the world as well?

While the story of the Singhs provides a personal glimpse into what the Lord is doing in the world, we must now take a macro-level look at his work. The rest of this chapter is an attempt to paint picture of migration on a large scale, noting figures across the world and specific matters related to the West.

ON MIGRATION NUMBERS, TABLES, AND CHARLIE BROWN'S TEACHER

From my childhood I have fond memories of watching the Peanuts cartoons that would typically be shown every year during the holiday seasons. In fact, I now enjoy watching the same episodes with my children. One classic character in the world Charles Schultz created was the unseen school teacher. You never saw this person, but the children always responded to her whenever they were in her class. While her concealment remained a mystery to the television audience, the most startling aspect was the fact that we never heard her speak our language. Though the Peanuts characters always knew what she was saying, the only sound that came from the television speaker whenever she spoke was a staccato, muted-trumpet sound: *"Wwaaa-wwaaa, wwaaa, wwaaa-wwaaa, wwaaa!"* We knew the teacher was an important part of the comic story line, but for the most part we understood her to be boring, impractical, and incomprehensible.

It is my fear that the remaining section of this chapter and portions of the following chapters will remind you of Charlie Brown's teacher. While you understand that facts about migrations to Western nations are important and necessary for this book, you might find them boring, impractical, and incomprehensible. I pray that such would not be the case and that you would not gloss over the next few pages, but would read what is to come with the eyes and heart of a kingdom citizen.

It is not my intention in this book to weary you with a lot of statistics, but some data is necessary to paint the picture of what has been occurring on a global scale. While the rest of this chapter contains tables, percentages, and other numbers, do not allow such information to cause you to grow weary. Such facts represent the Mr.

inghs and Aunties for whom Jesus died. Such numbers give us a glimpse into what in the world God is doing.

GLOBAL MIGRATION TRENDS

Consider the following statistics:

- The total estimated number of international migrants in 2010 was expected to reach 214 million, about 3% of the world's population.

- From 1990 to 2010 the more developed regions were expected to gain 45 million international migrants, an increase of 55%.

- In 2010 international migrants were projected to account for 10% of the total population residing in those regions, up from 7.2% in 1990.

- In the less developed regions, the migrant population was expected to increase by 13 million (18%) from 1990–2010.

- Europe was expected to host almost 70 million international migrants by 2010, one-third of the global total; Asia 61 million; North America 50 million.

- The increase of migrant populations between 2000–2010 was expected to be the highest in North America (24%), Europe (21%), and Oceania (20%).

- Between 2000 and 2010 nine countries gained over a million international migrants each: the United States (8 million), Spain (4.6 million), Italy (2.3 million), Saudi Arabia (2.2 million), the United Kingdom (1.7 million), Canada (1.6 million), the Syrian Arab Republic (1.3 million), Jordan (1 million), and the United Arab Emirates (1 million).

- In 2010 Asia was expected to host 10.9 million refugees, making up 66% of the global number of refugees. Africa was expected to host 2.6 million (16% of global refugees), Europe 1.6 million refugees (10%); Northern America 730,000, and Latin America and the Caribbean 530,000.[4]

- In 2005 countries with at least twenty million inhabitants where international migrants constituted high proportions of the population included Australia (20%), Canada (19%), France (11%), Germany (12%), Saudi Arabia (26%), Spain (11%), Ukraine (15%), and the United States (13%).[5]

- From 2000 to 2007 the number of international students more than doubled to over two million. The main destination countries were the United States, the United Kingdom, Germany, France, and Australia. The greatest percentage increases occurred in New Zealand, Korea, the Netherlands, Greece, Spain, Italy, and Ireland.[6]

- In 2010 migrants comprised 14.2% of the total population in North America, 12.4% in Western Europe, 22% in Australia, 21.3% in Canada, 13.5% in the United States, and 10.4% in the United Kingdom.[7]

- By 2017 one Canadian in five could be a visible minority person.[8]

Across the globe, people are on the move, with some movements being voluntary while others are not. An examination of the twenty countries or areas with the highest numbers of international migrants in 2005 reveals that several of those nations have been designated as the Western world. The United States, Germany, France, Canada, United Kingdom, Spain, Australia, and Italy all make the top-twenty list. What is even more fascinating is that the United States accounts for over 20% of the world's migrants, but when the other seven Western locations are added, the percentage soars to 41% (see table 2.1).

Table 2.1 Twenty Countries/Areas with Highest Numbers of International Migrants, 2005[9]

Country or Area	Number of Migrants (millions)	Percentage of Total
United States	38.4	20.2
Russian Federation	12.1	6.4
Germany	10.1	5.3

Country or Area	Number of Migrants (millions)	Percentage of Total
Ukraine	6.8	3.6
France	6.5	3.4
Saudi Arabia	6.4	3.3
Canada	6.1	3.2
India	5.7	3.0
United Kingdom	5.4	2.8
Spain	4.8	2.5
Australia	4.1	2.2
Pakistan	3.3	1.7
United Arab Emirates	3.2	1.7
China, Hong Kong SAR	3.0	1.6
Israel	2.7	1.4
Italy	2.5	1.3
Kazakhstan	2.5	1.3
Cote d'Ivoire	2.4	1.2
Jordan	2.2	1.2
Japan	2.0	1.1

To provide a sense of comparison over the past few years, table 2.2 displays the ten nations with the highest estimated numbers of international migrants in 2010 and their corresponding percentages of the global total. While there is some variation, six of the top ten are Western countries.

Table 2.2 Countries with Highest Numbers of International Migrants, 2010[10]

Country	Estimated Number of International Migrants, Mid 2010	Percentage of Global Total
United States	42,813,281	20
Russian Federation	12,270,388	5.7
Germany	10,758,061	5
Saudi Arabia	7,288,900	3.4
Canada	7,202,340	3.4
France	6,684,842	3.1
United Kingdom	6,451,711	3
Spain	6,377,524	3
India	5,436,012	2.5
Ukraine	5,257,527	2.5

Migration is taking place in every region of the world. However, certain regions have higher concentrations than others. In 2005 one out of every three international migrants lived in Europe, and one out of every four international migrants lived in Northern America. Between 1990 and 2005 the proportion of international migrants living in Europe rose from 32 to 34 percent. During this same period the proportion living in Northern America increased from 18 to 23 percent, the fastest growth rate of any region.[11] While significant migration occurs in Africa, Asia, and Latin America, the focus of this book is on the areas of the world that have historically contained Western lands.

MIGRATION TO NORTH AMERICA

Of the countries and territories that comprise North America, by far the United States and Canada receive the most migrants. The governments of these nations attempt to keep an accurate account of the different people groups who migrate to their lands. At present, numerous debates on a variety of topics related to migration are occurring in these two countries.

Canada. The data collected from the 2006 Canadian census revealed that migration is alive and well in this northernmost North American country. The portion of the country's population born outside of Canada reached its highest level in seventy-five years, with 6,186,950 people. This amounted to 19.8% of the total population, the highest proportion since 1931.[12]

Between 2001 and 2006, 14% of those migrating to the country came from the People's Republic of China. Migrants from India were next in line with 11.6% of the total migrants. These were followed by the Philippines (7%), Pakistan (5.2%), South Korea (3.2%), and Iran (2.5%). In 2006 almost 150 languages were reported as a mother tongue among the foreign-born population. The largest portion reported Chinese (18.6%) as their heart language, followed by Italian (6.6%), Punjabi (5.9%), Spanish (5.8%),

German (5.4%), Tagalog (4.8%), and Arabic (4.7%).[13]

Instead of migrating to Canada and looking for land to farm, contemporary migrants are predominantly urbanites and are even more likely to live in a metropolitan area than Canadian-born citizens. In 2006, 94.9% of the foreign-born population and 97.2% of the recent immigrants lived in either a census metropolitan area or a census agglomeration (i.e., urban community), as compared with 77.5% of the Canadian-born citizens. Toronto, Montreal, and Vancouver received 68.9% (765,000) of migrants between 2001 and 2006, while only 2.8% decided to live in rural areas.[14]

In the four Atlantic provinces, Halifax, Nova Scotia, boasted the largest foreign-born population, receiving over five thousand immigrants, with just over half (51.4%) being born in Asia and the Middle East. Montreal, Quebec, was declared home to Canada's third-largest foreign-born population. Of the 740,400 people in the foreign-born population, 31% came from Asia and the Middle East. Six of the ten leading birthplaces were naturally from countries where French is spoken: Algeria (8.7%), Morocco (7.6%), Romania (7.2%), France (6.3%), Haiti (5.2%), and Lebanon (3.2%). Toronto is the country's largest migrant-receiving area, with the 2006 census noting 2,320,200 foreign-born people. The foreign-born population is now at 45.7% of the census metropolitan area's total population of 5,072,100, with India and the People's Republic of China as the two major-source countries for recent immigrants.[15]

In Hamilton almost 25% of the population is foreign born. Between 2001 and 2006 the foreign-born population grew by 7.7%, with the total population of the Hamilton census metropolitan area increasing by 4.3%. For Winnipeg the Philippines is the number one source for recent immigrants. In Calgary the foreign-born population is growing faster than the Canadian-born population. Vancouver is the major point of entry for immigrants to the western part of the country. Between 2001 and 2006 the foreign-born population

of Vancouver grew five times faster than the Canadian-born population, with most of the new migrants born in Asia and the Middle
East. The foreign-born population in the city now accounts for
45.6% of the total population, almost equivalent to that of Toronto.[16]

It is predicted that by 2017 about 20% of Canada's population
could be visible minorities, anywhere from 6.3 million to 8.5 million
people. Half of this growth is expected to come from South Asian or
Chinese peoples, with the highest growth rates coming from West
Asian, Korean, and Arab groups.[17]

United States. Though the Native Americans had migrated and
had been living in what is now the United States long before Europeans, the last five hundred years of America's history has been a history
containing waves of international migrants originally coming primarily
from European nations and as slaves from Africa. Recent migrants
have arrived mainly from Asia and Latin America. Of all the countries
throughout the world receiving migrants, the United States by far leads
the way with the largest numbers and percentage received. By 2010 the
US international migrant population reached an estimated 43 million,
representing approximately 13.5 percent of the total population.[18]

Large numbers of Asians migrated to America after the 1965 Immigration Act, with one-third of all US immigrants now coming
from that continent. Their numbers increased dramatically across
the twentieth century, from 17,000 in 1965 to more than 250,000
annually in the 1980s and over 300,000 per year in the early 1990s.[19]

By 2010, the largest numbers of legal permanent residents of the
United States came from the following countries:

Table 2.3 2010 Legal Permanent US Resident Status by Country of Birth[20]

Mexico	139,120
China, People's Republic	70,863
India	69,162
Philippines	58,173
Dominican Republic	53,870

Cuba	33,573
Vietnam	30,632
Haiti	22,582
Colombia	22,406
Korea, South	22,227
Iraq	19,855
Jamaica	19,825
El Salvador	18,806
Pakistan	18,258
Bangladesh	14,819
Ethiopia	14,266
Peru	14,247
Iran	14,182
Nigeria	13,376
Canada	13,328
All other countries	359,055

Refugees. Each year large numbers of refugees enter the United States. During the 1990s refugee arrivals averaged over one hundred thousand each year, with a decline in the early twenty-first century. There was a 25 percent increase in the numbers of such people admitted from 2007 (48,218) to 2008 (60,108).[21] The following table displays the numbers of a few select refugee arrivals by country of nationality in 2010 to the United States, including the total number of refugees to arrive that year.

Table 2.4 2010 Refugee Arrivals to the US by Country of Nationality[22]

Iraq	18,016
Burma	16,693
Bhutan	12,363
Somalia	4,884
Cuba	4,818
Iran	3,543
Congo, Democratic Republic	3,174
Eritrea	2,570
Vietnam	873
Ethiopia	668
All other countries, including unknown	5,691
Total	**73,293**

Students. Postsecondary school students are another source adding to the multiethnic composition of the United States. In 2010-2011, students from the top five countries of China (21.8%), India (14.4%), South Korea (10.1%), Canada (3.8%) and Taiwan (3.4%), made up over 53% of all international students in the United States. Large annual percent increases occurred among the number of students from China (23.5%) and Saudi Arabia (43.6%), while the number of students from Japan decreased by 14%. The following table shows the top twenty-five leading places of origin of international students to the United States.

Table 2.5 Top Twenty-Five Places of Origin of International Students in the United States[23]

Rank	Place of Origin	2009/10	2010/11	% of Total	% Change
	WORLD TOTAL	690,923	723,277	100.0	4.7
1	China	127,628	157,558	21.8	23.5
2	India	104,897	103,895	14.4	-1.0
3	South Korea	72,153	73,351	10.1	1.7
4	Canada	28,145	27,546	3.8	-2.1
5	Taiwan	26,685	24,818	3.4	-7.0
6	Saudi Arabia	15,810	22,704	3.1	43.6
7	Japan	24,842	21,290	2.9	-14.3
8	Vietnam	13,112	14,888	2.1	13.5
9	Mexico	13,450	13,713	1.9	2.0
10	Turkey	12,397	12,184	1.7	-1.7
11	Nepal	11,233	10,301	1.4	-8.3
12	Germany	9,548	9,458	1.3	-0.9
13	United Kingdom	8,861	8,947	1.2	1.0
14	Brazil	8,786	8,777	1.2	-0.1
15	Thailand	8,531	8,236	1.1	-3.5
16	Hong Kong	8,034	8,136	1.1	1.3
17	France	7,716	8,098	1.1	5.0
18	Nigeria	6,568	7,148	1.0	8.8
19	Indonesia	6,943	6,942	1.0	0.0
20	Malaysia	6,190	6,735	0.9	8.8
21	Colombia	6,920	6,456	0.9	-6.7
22	Iran	4,731	5,626	0.8	18.9
23	Venezuela	4,958	5,491	0.8	10.8
24	Pakistan	5,222	5,045	0.7	-3.4
25	Russia	4,827	4,692	0.6	-2.8

MIGRATIONS TO WESTERN EUROPE

Mass migrations from Europe marked the nineteenth and twentieth centuries. Yet the demographic landscape is different today, with many European nations receiving large numbers of migrants. The social and cultural landscape of Europe has been experiencing seismic shifts in recent years, with migration being a contributing factor to the changes. This trend is so extensive that Jan A. B. Jongeneel observed that "many European politicians do not like to admit that nowadays Europe has more or less become an immigrant continent."[24]

By 2010 it was estimated that Western Europe had twenty-three million international migrants, comprising 12.4% of the population. In France 10.7% of the population consisted of international migrants. In Germany that proportion was 13.1%; in Belgium, 9.1%; in Spain, 14.1%; and in the United Kingdom, 10.4%.[25] A cursory glance at table 2.1 and table 2.2 (presented previously) reveals several areas of Western Europe containing some of the world's largest numbers of international migrants. In 2005 Germany had the third-largest number in the world, followed by France (5th), the United Kingdom (9th), Spain (10th), Italy (16th), Switzerland (26th), and the Netherlands (28th). Europe is also the destination for approximately 85 percent of migrants from North Africa.[26]

Here are a few specific locations to serve as an illustration of the migrations of peoples to Western Europe.

United Kingdom. An estimated 577,000 people arrived in the United Kingdom in 2007 to live for at least one year.[27] In 2009, the number of people granted British citizenship was 203,790. While people from various nations migrated to this area of the world, India and Pakistan provided the largest number of people.[28] The following table provides a glimpse of the numbers and countries of previous nationality for 2009.

Table 2.6 Top 2009 Grants of British Citizenship in the UK by Previous Nationality[29]

India	26,535
Pakistan	20,945
Bangladesh	12,040
Philippines	11,750
South Africa	8,365
Somalia	8,140
Zimbabwe	7,705
Turkey	7,205
Nigeria	6,955
China	6,335
Other previous nationalities	87,730

Italy. Between 1981 and 1991 the number of foreigners with residence permits in Italy doubled, from three hundred thousand to six hundred thousand. By 2004 the total foreign population increased to 2.4 million people.[30] By 2008 the total registered foreign population reached 3.9 million. The number of non-Italian students and asylum seekers increased as well. Inflows of the top nationalities as a percentage of all foreigners in 2008 were from Morocco, Albania, Ukraine, Moldova, China, India, Bangladesh, Philippines, Sri Lanka, and Brazil.[31]

Spain. In nine years, from 1990 to 1999, the foreign population grew from 279,000 to 801,000.[32] In 2006 more than 800,000 foreigners migrated to Spain. This number was 17% higher than the total in 2005.[33] By 2008 the foreign-born population was 14.1% of the total population, compared to 4.9% in 2000. Inflows of the top nationalities as a percentage of all foreigners were from Morocco, Romania, Colombia, Ecuador, Peru, Brazil, China, the United Kingdom, Paraguay, and Italy.[34]

France. By 2005 the foreign-born population reached almost 5 million people, comprising 8.1% of the country's total population.[35] In 2006 Africa was the largest-sending continent, followed by Asia. One-third of new immigrants arrived from Algeria and Morocco.[36]

The next eight top-sending nations included Turkey, Tunisia, Cameroon, China, the Democratic Republic of Congo, Côte d'Ivoire, Mali, and Haiti.[37] The number of foreign students was up to 49,750 in 2008, with the primary countries of origin being China, Morocco, Algeria, Tunisia, and the United States. The number of foreign students from China has increased at an average annual rate of over 30% for the last thirteen years. The number of asylum applications rose to 42,600 in 2008, with 36% receiving refugee status.[38]

Germany. During the early part of the twenty-first century, the estimated total number of foreign-born people living in Germany was 9.7 million.[39] As of 2003 the foreign-born population was 10,621,000, or roughly 12.9% of the total population.[40] By 2006 the top-sending nations included Poland, Turkey, Romania, Hungary, Italy, the Russian Federation, United States, China, France, and the Slovak Republic.[41] By 2007 the inflow of foreign populations into the country reached almost 575,000 people.[42] Asylum requests rose by 23% from 2008 to 2009. And international students numbered 58,400 in 2008, up from 45,700 in the year 2000.[43]

Austria. Recent changes in Austria's immigration laws have influenced migration. While the 2006 inflow of foreigners was below the previous year, 85,400 people migrated to Austria. During the same year 26,300 foreigners were naturalized, with 50% of those people coming from the successor states of the former Yugoslavia and another 30% coming from Turkey. The top-sending countries to Austria in 2006 were Germany, Serbia and Montenegro, Poland, Turkey, Romania, Hungary, the Slovak Republic, Bosnia and Herzegovina, Croatia, and Italy.[44] By 2008 the migration of foreign nationals increased to 95,000. In that same year there were 8,500 new international students, almost three times the amount in 2005 (3,200). Over the past decade Austria has been one of the main destination countries for asylum seekers.[45]

Belgium. While over half of the eighty-three thousand foreigners who migrated to Belgium in 2006 were from European Union countries, some of the other highest percentages also came from Morocco, Romania, and Turkey. Migration during this year was 8 percent higher than in 2005 and was the highest recorded level for over twenty years.[46]

MIGRATIONS TO OCEANIA

The two major traditional strongholds of Western civilization in Oceania are Australia and New Zealand. While Japan is often referred to as a westernized country and is clearly one of the world's leading postindustrialized nations, its general cultural values still reflect an Eastern worldview and way of life. Traditionally, it has clearly not been described as a Western country. For these reasons the focus of this section of the world will be on Australia and New Zealand.

These two countries experienced an increase in the number of international migrants in the latter part of the twentieth century and in the early twenty-first century. The number rose from 4.1 million in 1990 to 5.7 million by 2010. As a percentage of the population, the number rose from 20% (1990) to 22% (2010).[47]

Australia. Migration now contributes over half of Australia's population growth, making it one of the world's most multiethnic countries. From 2006 to 2007 almost 230,000 visas were granted to overseas students, a 20% increase from the previous year.[48] There were 206,135 permanent visas issued in 2007–2008. This number reflects a 9% increase when compared to the previous year and does not include the number of New Zealanders settling in the country.[49] It is estimated that around 44% of all Australians were either born overseas or have at least one parent who was born overseas.[50] Of the top-ten source countries from 2006 to 2007 (aside from the top two—U.K. and New Zealand), the majority of the migrants were from China, India, Philippines, Malaysia, Korea, and Singapore (South Africa and Sudan were also in the top ten).[51] From 2006 to 2007, 1,300 visas were provided for refugees and humanitarian needs, with Sudan, Myanmar, Iraq, and Afghanistan being the main source countries for refugees.[52] From 2008 to 2009 the number of offshore student visas rose 15% (227,900) as compared to the previous year.[53]

Table 2.7 Top 2010–2011 Permanent Additions to Australia by Country of Birth[54]

Birthplace	2010-2011 Total
China (excl. SARs and Taiwan)	29,397
New Zealand	25,787
India	21,932
United Kingdom	20,581
Philippines	11,075
South Africa	9,230
Vietnam	5,060
Sri Lanka	5,014
Malaysia	5,004
Korea	4,405
Iran	3,763
Iraq	3,502
Afghanistan	3,202
Ireland	3,029
Thailand	2,931
United States	2,918
Indonesia	2,887
Nepal	2,406
Bangladesh	2,274
Pakistan	2,143
Zimbabwe	2,069
Hong Kong	1,967
Fiji	1,872
Singapore	1,823
Germany	1,712
Total All Countries	**213,409**

New Zealand. The 2001 census revealed that 19.5% of all New Zealanders were born overseas, with almost 28% having lived in the country for less than five years.[55] From 2006 to 2007 approximately 47,000 people were approved for residence in the country, with the largest-source countries being the United Kingdom (26%), China (12%), India (9%), and South Africa (8%). During this time approximately 67,100 student permits were granted.[56] Between April 2008 and April 2009, 64,500 permanent/long-term, non-New Zealand citizens arrived in the country.[57] From 2008 to 2009, 73,926 international students were approved for study, a 6% increase from the 2007–2008 period. While there was a decline in the number of Chinese students, the number of students from other countries, such as India, offset the decrease. The country recently entered into agreements with the Philippines and Vietnam, allowing highly skilled professionals to enter its labor market.[58]

CONCLUSION

While the statistics may appear overwhelming, they reveal that many of the world's peoples are arriving annually in the Western countries of the world. Many are coming from countries with large numbers of unreached and least reached people groups. While some of these numbers represent the migration of kingdom citizens, others represent people who do not know the Creator. Yes, the Lord is bringing the Mr. Singhs and Aunties into our communities. Yes, the challenges are great, but the Great Commission opportunity is even greater. Prayerfully join with me now as we continue to examine migration from a kingdom perspective, addressing biblical, historical, and missional matters. It is my prayer that what is learned in our journey together will allow you to have a part in knowing that you contributed to the nations walking in the light of the glory of the Lord (Revelation 21:22–27).

The World's Unreached in the West

PEOPLES ON THE MOVE

It has been called British Columbia's Highway to Heaven. Number 5 Road that runs through Richmond, south of Vancouver, is lined with more than twenty places of worship, including Sikh, Muslim, and Hindu structures. The first traditional Tibetan Buddhist monastery in the Pacific Northwest is also located along that road, as is the growing Ling Yen Mountain Temple. Over 60 percent of the city's approximately 190,000 residents are of Chinese or South Asian origins.[1]

■ ■ ■

IN 1974 MISSIOLOGIST RALPH WINTER brought the concept of an unreached people group (UPG) to the forefront of the minds of most evangelicals with his presentation "The Highest Priority: Cross-Cultural Evangelism" at the International Congress on World Evangelization held in Lausanne, Switzerland. Now, almost forty years later, phrases such as *unreached* and *least reached* peoples are common parlance among evangelicals.

At the time of this writing, there are 11,642 people groups in the world.[2] Out of this number, 6,734 people groups are comprised of less than 2 percent evangelicals, providing them the label *unreached*. In terms of the global population, the unreached peoples make up over four billion individuals.[3] In this chapter I wish to provide you with a glimpse of the world's unreached peoples who are living in the West. However, before we are able to note these groups and their numbers, it is important to understand the sources of our data.

WHERE THE NUMBERS COME FROM

At present there are three main sets of data on the total number of the world's UPGs: World Christian Database,[4] Joshua Project,[5] and the Global Research Department of the International Mission Board (Global Research).[6] These databases represent years of research and are very impressive collections. They are great blessings to the church.

While researchers representing each of these databases collaborate with one another to share and discuss their data and updates, each collection differs in degrees related to certain definitions, philosophies, and missiological and theological convictions. Joshua Project's website offers some insight as to why there are three different lists:

> How many countries are there in the world? The answer depends on who you ask. Should there only be one list of countries in the world? Different perspectives on the same situation are a healthy thing. Looking at a picture from several angles often yields greater appreciation. Using different definitions and criteria can help clarify a task and highlight areas needing further research. People group database compilers are confronted by questions such as: Is language always the primary definer of a people group? Should caste be considered when defining a people group? Should Christian Adherents be considered when setting the criterion for unreached? Should unreached be defined by exposure or response to the Gospel? What are acceptable sources for input and edits? The three global peoples lists answer these questions slightly differently and thus provide different but valuable perspectives.[7]

For the purposes of this book, I have chosen to use the data from Joshua Project and that from the Global Research Department of the International Mission Board. Both of these sources are readily available to the public, often cited, well-respected, and frequently updated.[8]

WHAT IS *UNREACHED*?

People-group researchers study, among other things, the percentage of evangelicals among people groups, because their distinction between a *reached* and an *unreached* people has much to do with the concentration of evangelicals present. Both Joshua Project and the International Mission Board hold to the same definition of *evangelical*. Joshua Project's website notes that evangelicals are followers of Christ who generally emphasize the Lord Jesus Christ as the sole source of salvation through faith in him, personal faith and conversion with regeneration by the Holy Spirit, a recognition of the inspired Word of God as the only basis for faith and living, and commitment to biblical preaching and evangelism that brings others to faith in Christ.[9]

Joshua Project's definition of an unreached people group is one that is less than 2% evangelical *and* less than 5% "Christian Adherent."[10] Therefore, if a group was 1.5% evangelical but 10% of the group labeled themselves as Christian, Joshua Project would consider that group reached. The International Mission Board's definition of an unreached people group is similar to that of Joshua Project but without the Christian Adherent percentage. Their website states that an unreached people group is one in which less than 2% of the population are evangelical Christians.[11] While researchers with each organization differ on other matters, such as general definitions of all people groups, for our purposes their distinction between reached and unreached is important to keep in mind.

A DISCLAIMER

The purpose of this chapter is simply to note the large numbers of the world's unreached people groups residing in Western countries. As much as possible, I want to help you to see the countries and the diversity represented within them. A significant means of doing this is to share with you the data from two of the world's most respected resources on UPGs.

While I am familiar with the reasons for the discrepancies between the numbers and recognize that the use of the term *Christian Adherents* factors into the different totals, I am not convinced that the numerical differences are simply a matter of definition as to how we should categorize a people group. Yet having stated these concerns, I am not attempting to pit one organization against the other. So while the differences between the two sources will be noticeable, the purpose of this chapter is to raise awareness of the unreached-people-group realities in the West and the lack of accurate data for the United States and Canada. It is my hope and prayer that future researchers will be able to provide more accurate data. The people have moved in next door, and for the most part they are strangers to us.

MEJRA: A STRANGER NEXT DOOR

One example of the multitudes of unreached peoples migrating to the West is Mejra. I met her at the usual place where I get my hair cut. She was the first Bosnian I had met, and I was later able to share the love of Jesus with her. I learned that she and her family had fled the war in Bosnia to Germany. After spending some time there, they eventually were allowed to immigrate to the United States. Now she and her husband and teenage children are on the list of the almost 109,000 Bosnians living in this country.[12]

Mejra is a Muslim and has a heart for her country and people. She loves her culture and food. She makes certain her children know her heart language in addition to English. Since the conflict has subsided in Bosnia, she and her children return to visit family. Last year her children spent their summer vacation in Bosnia, staying with relatives. The global evangelical status of the Bosnian people is less than 2 percent, making them one of the world's unreached peoples—at the time of this writing. In the West the Bosnians are located in the following countries:

Table 3.1 Bosnian Locations and Estimated Populations in the West (Global Research)[13]

Canada	13,178
France	100
Germany	286,000
Ireland	888
Italy	29,000
United Kingdom	2,000
United States	108,924

And while locations and population numbers differ between Global Research and Joshua Project (see table 3.2), both of these data sources point to the location of a large number of Bosnians scattered across Western countries.

Table 3.2 Bosnian Locations and Estimated Populations in the West (Joshua Project)[14]

Austria	77,000
Germany	284,000
Italy	3,600
Norway	15,000
Sweden	54,000
Switzerland	116,000
United States	111,000

What can the Lord do with one person like Mejra who is tightly connected with the Bosnian communities in the United States and in Bosnia? Could the gospel travel across her social networks among the Bosnians living in the United States and in Bosnia? While the Bosnians are one of the world's unreached peoples living next door to us, who else is in our neighborhoods, and what are their numbers?

JAY: A STRANGER NEXT DOOR

I met Jay in a coffee shop in Old Louisville, a historic area of my city. A friend and I were on a church-planting team and were in the community each week doing evangelism. While waiting for our drinks, I heard a voice behind me exclaim, "He's crazy!" I turned around and noticed a young Palestinian man standing there in shock, looking at the front page of *The New York Times*. I asked him what was the matter. As he pointed to a picture of a Muslim cleric in the Middle East, he told me the cleric was attempting to lead an uprising and cause great trouble.

My friend and I introduced ourselves to Jay and welcomed him to drink his tea with us. After spending some time in conversation together, we were able to share the gospel with him. Jay was a first-generation immigrant to the United States. And although he was Muslim, he wanted to meet with us over the next six weeks in the coffee shop to talk about Jesus. Jay did not come to faith in Jesus during that time, but he was very open to hearing about the good news.

The percentage of evangelicals among Arab Palestinians in several countries in the world is less than 2 percent. If Jay does come to faith in Jesus, is it not possible that the Lord could use him to take the gospel to other Palestinians in Israel, Jordan, and Lebanon?

HOW MANY UPGS ARE IN THE WEST?

Table 3.3 Unreached Peoples in the West (Joshua Project and Global Research)[15]

Country	UPGs, Joshua Project	UPGs, Joshua Project (with Adherent % Removed)	UPGs, Global Research
Andorra	3	9	5
Australia	11	36	43
Austria	6	34	23
Belgium	10	26	34
Canada	41	132	180
Denmark	12	22	20
Finland	7	18	6

Country	UPGs, Joshua Project	UPGs, Joshua Project (with Adherent % Removed)	UPGs, Global Research
France	34	79	97
Germany	19	57	64
Greenland	–	3	1
Iceland	1	5	4
Ireland	4	13	10
Italy	12	50	48
Liechtenstein	2	6	3
Luxembourg	2	13	10
Malta	3	7	5
Monaco	1	8	6
Netherlands	13	45	41
New Zealand	6	23	21
Norway	14	41	11
Portugal	5	16	22
San Marino	–	4	2
Spain	7	40	37
Sweden	8	38	28
Switzerland	6	21	18
United Kingdom	29	66	73
United States	73	242	361
TOTAL:	**329**	**1054**	**1173**

Table 3.3 displays the numbers of unreached peoples living in Western countries as tallied by Joshua Project and Global Research. Since the latter organization defines an unreached people group as less than 2% evangelical, I decided for comparison's sake to also show Joshua Project numbers, if a similar definition is used for the peoples in each country. Joshua Project notes that 329 unreached people groups reside in the West as compared to 1,173 unreached people according to Global Research. However, the number from Joshua Project increases to 1,054 when the percentage of adherents to Christianity is not taken into consideration.

Since the Bible defines a believer as someone who has experienced a regenerative work of the Holy Spirit resulting in repentance and faith in Jesus and not simply a traditional or cultural adherence to Christianity, I subscribe to the less-than-2% definition of Global Research. For example, according to Joshua Project, in Spain the French are 0.5% evangelical, the Portuguese are 0.13% evangelical, and the Spaniards are 0.4% evangelical, yet because these peoples have come from Christianized lands—and would describe themselves as Christians—they are not counted as unreached people groups. While I recognize the strategic reasons Joshua Project subscribes to defining an unreached people in consideration of their adherent level, theologically and missiologically I am not comfortable with such a guideline. Therefore, I believe it is possible to come to a better approximation of the number of unreached peoples in the West by comparing the third and fourth columns in table 3.3. While additional limitations will be noted in the next section, the number of unreached peoples living in the West is likely to fall between 329 and 1,173. Clearly, this is a wide range, and one that is not very helpful. Since I am more concerned about evangelical percentages than simply those who adhere to the Christian tradition, my estimation is that the more accurate count is somewhere between 1,054 and 1,173 unreached people groups living in the West.

THE X FACTORS:
THE UNITED STATES AND CANADA

The irony is that while the United States and Canada are two of the most researched counties in the world, the present data on these nations regarding the number of unreached peoples are very limited. For the most part, Joshua Project has spent the majority of its time focused on countries other than the United States and Canada, where access to the gospel is more limited. In a recent conversation with Dan Scribner, director of Joshua Project, I was told that the data for these two countries is representative but not comprehensive. While the information is a starting point for understanding present realities, it is based primarily on census data and does not provide the details for an accurate understanding of the people groups. In other words, just because Afghanis show up in a national count, the research has not been accomplished to provide the people groups in this nationality.

I received a similar response from Jim Haney, director of Global Research. At the time of this writing, Global Research has the assignment of researching through their field researchers and other partners every country of the world *except* the United States and Canada. And because their research has been focused elsewhere, they are not confident of providing accurate people-group counts or evangelical percentages of the various peoples living in these two countries or information about whether anyone is engaging such peoples with the gospel and planting churches among them. Despite this limitation, Global Research is able to provide the names and estimated populations of several hundred unreached peoples residing in the United States and Canada (see appendix 1). However, the status of these as unreached is based on the assumption that since the same people groups are unreached in other countries of the world, then it is highly likely that those same people groups are unreached in the United States and Canada.

According to Southern Baptist Convention (the denomination connected to the Global Research Department of the International Mission Board) policy, the North American Mission Board is assigned to missionary activity in the United States, Canada, and their respective territories. Unfortunately, very little research has been conducted by the North American Mission Board on their assigned region of the world.

Therefore, at the time of this writing, accurate information on the UPGs living in the United States and Canada does not exist. Not only do we not know who is living in our communities, we do not know their evangelical statuses or who may be working among them as church planters. The data does not exist because the research has never been conducted. *We have better data on a UPG living on the backside of the Himalayas than we do on that same people group living across the street from us in New York, Toronto, Chicago, or Montreal.* This is a pathetic reality and reflective of much of the missiology found in this part of North America.

While better research and more accurate data are needed, I believe it is possible to make some assumptions based on the limited information available. Table 3.4 shows the data from table 3.3 but for Canada and the United States only. By comparing both sets of data, we can make some important assumptions.

Table 3.4 Unreached Peoples in Canada and the United States (Joshua Project and Global Research)[16]

Country	UPGs, Joshua Project	UPGs, Joshua Project (with Adherent % Removed)	UPGs, Global Research
Canada	41	132	180
United States	73	242	361
TOTAL:	**114**	**374**	**541**

First, there is a large discrepancy between the data sets for these two countries. With as much migration as happens within these nations, future priority must be given to research in this part of North America. Second, there are several hundred people groups living in these countries that represent people groups that have been identified as unreached in other countries—including other Western countries. Third, if the evangelical percentages of these peoples in other nations are similar to those same peoples in the United States and Canada, then there is a strong probability that they are unreached in these two North American countries as well. While I recognize this statement may not be the case, it is an assumption based on global realities. And until accurate data is provided for the United States and Canada, I believe it is safe to assume such a degree of lostness until proven otherwise.

THE GLOBAL PICTURE

Before providing the names of the unreached peoples living in the West, we need to zoom out and get a bigger picture of reality. Table 3.5 shows the forty countries with the largest numbers of unreached peoples according to both Global Research and the seventh edition of *Operation World*.[17]

Table 3.5 Countries with Highest Numbers of Unreached Peoples[18]

Countries with the Largest Number of Unreached Peoples, Global Research			Countries with the Largest Number of Unreached Peoples, *Operation World* (7th ed).		
Rank	Country	Number of People Groups	Rank	Country	Unreached People Groups
1	India	941	1	India	2,223
2	China	368	2	China, PRC	427
3	United States	361	3	Pakistan	374
4	Brazil	187	4	Bangladesh	353
5	Canada	180	5	Nepal	325
6	Indonesia	177	6	Indonesia	200
7	Mexico	161	7	Sudan	138
8	Sudan	153	8	Laos	134
9	Congo, D. R.	153	9	Iran	93
10	Nigeria	121	10	Russia	77
11	Chad	114	11	Thailand	75
12	Cameroon	114	12	Chad	72
13	Ethiopia	108	13	Afghanistan	71
14	Laos	101	14	Nigeria	67
15	Tanzania	100	15	Sri Lanka	64
16	France	97	16	Vietnam	63
17	Nepal	96	17	United States	59
18	Pakistan	87	18	Brazil	58
19	South Sudan	86	19	Malaysia	56
20	Colombia	79	20	Myanmar	51
21	Russia	75	21	Kazakhstan	41
22	United Kingdom	73	22	Israel	40
23	Myanmar	66	23	Turkey	38
24	Zambia	65	24	Mali	37
25	Germany	64	25	Uzbekistan	37
26	Iran	64	26	Algeria	35

Countries with the Largest Number of Unreached Peoples, Global Research			Countries with the Largest Number of Unreached Peoples, *Operation World* (7th ed).		
Rank	Country	Number of People Groups	Rank	Country	Unreached People Groups
27	Congo	61	27	Kenya	35
28	Malaysia	54	28	Côte d'Ivoire	34
29	Burkina Faso	53	29	Tanzania	33
30	Uzbekistan	52	30	France	33
31	Uganda	51	31	Bhutan	32
32	Central African Republic	50	32	Cambodia	30
33	Vietnam	48	33	Guinea	29
34	Benin	48	34	Burkina Faso	28
35	Italy	48	35	Libya	28
36	Turkey	46	36	Niger	28
37	Afghanistan	45	37	United Kingdom	28
38	Kenya	44	38	Senegal	27
39	Mozambique	43	39	Kyrgyzstan	27
40	Kazakhstan	43	40	Tajikistan	27
41	Australia	43			

There are a few important matters worthy of our attention from this table. First, while the lists differ in significant ways, it is important to recognize that peoples from many of these countries have migrated to Western nations. These migrants should be seen as potential bridges into their countries of birth as well as into other Western countries where their people may be found. For example, while several Western countries do not show up on this table, sizeable numbers of peoples from Bangladesh, Russia, Nepal, Guinea, and Senegal have migrated to those nations.

Second, traditionally Western countries are represented on this table. So, even among the countries with the highest numbers of unreached peoples, researchers find Western nations. It should be noted that the United States shows up in both lists. According to Global Research, the United States and Canada are included among the top five countries with the largest number of unreached people groups.

Finally, more Western countries would be added to the Operation World list, and it is likely their rankings would be higher, if the "less than 2% evangelical" definition was used for what constitutes an unreached people group. Since the data from Operation World follows closely with that of Joshua Project, naturally several Western countries are not included.

WHO ARE THE UPGS AND WHERE ARE THEY FOUND IN THE WEST?

It is one matter to be provided the big picture by looking at table 3.5, and it is another matter to inquire as to who are the unreached peoples living in the West and their locations. Because the tables from both Joshua Project and Global Research are several pages in length, they are placed as appendices in this book. Here is what you will find:

- Appendix 1: Unreached People Groups in the United States and Canada (Global Research)

- Appendix 2: Unreached People Groups in the West, Excluding the United States and Canada (Global Research)

- Appendix 3: Unreached People Groups in the West (Joshua Project)

I want to strongly encourage you to take a moment to examine the numbers of peoples on these tables found in Western countries. As you look over the appendices, note the locations of the peoples who have migrated from most of the countries found in table 3.5.

CONCLUSION

Many of the world's unreached people groups are living in Western countries. Some of these groups are comprised of large numbers; others are not so large. Regardless, the church must recognize the Great Commission opportunity set before her. History contains stories of people coming to faith in Jesus while outside their homeland, only to return home and share this good news. Some have returned to be martyred for the love of Jesus; others have experienced the multiplication of disciples, pastors, and churches through their evangelism. The Lord of the harvest has used them all to advance the gospel and his glory as the church waits for the Bridegroom to return.

The Lord may be planning to use the stranger next door to you to take the gospel to a people group that you will never see or encounter. Will you reach out to the stranger?

Migration and Kingdom Expansion
Part 1

PEOPLES ON THE MOVE

It has been called America's Muslim capitol. It is estimated that 40% of the one hundred thousand residents of Dearborn, Michigan, identify themselves as Arab Americans. East Dearborn is mainly Lebanese. Over the years, Palestinian immigrants helped change Dearborn from a "Christian" working-class neighborhood to a growing Muslim professional area. Southend is mostly comprised of Yemenis. Many of the Yemeni men migrated to the community without their families. They are less educated and less fluent in English than the other Muslim immigrants. These men frequently go back to Yemen but plan to return there permanently. Along the northern border with Detroit, almost ten thousand Iraqis formed a close community after being granted asylum in the United States, fleeing Saddam Hussein after the 1991 Gulf War.[1]

■   ■   ■

BEFORE CONTINUING OUR DISCUSSION of contemporary migrations, it is important that we examine the Scriptures to observe how the Sovereign Lord has worked through the migration of his people to work out his plan in the world. Whether migration was the result of sinful behavior or willful obedience, the Lord was engaged through the movement of peoples to fulfill salvation history. This chapter examines select passages in the Old Testament that provide a biblical and theological foundation for how we should understand and respond to global migrations in light of the Great Commission.

Even though I noted in chapter 1 that God is sovereign over peoples' histories and locations so that they may come to know him (Acts 17:26–27), the reality of his intimate involvement with the movement of the nations also is revealed throughout the Old Testament. And such movements, while they may be difficult and tragic at times, are part of a purpose in bringing the gospel to the nations that they might come to know their Savior.

MIGRATION BEFORE THE FALL

The migration of peoples across the world was not an afterthought in the mind of God when Adam and Eve sinned. For even in the first chapter of Genesis, immediately after the creation of man and woman, God blessed them and said, "Be fruitful and multiply and *fill the earth* and subdue it and have dominion over the fish of the sea and over the birds of the heavens and over every living thing that moves on the earth" (Genesis 1:28, emphasis added). What began as one man and one woman was to become a global population scattered across the third planet from the sun. The point is clear that through procreation and movement, the migration of peoples to fill the earth for God's glory was stated from the beginning.

MIGRATION FROM THE GARDEN

The first migration of people from their home is observed in Genesis and is the result of the sinful behavior of Adam and Eve:

> Then the LORD God said, "Behold, the man has become like one of us in knowing good and evil. Now, lest he reach out his hand and take also of the tree of life and eat, and live forever—" therefore the LORD God sent him out from the garden of Eden to work the ground from which he was taken. He drove out the

man, and at the east of the garden of Eden he placed the cherubim and a flaming sword that turned every way to guard the way to the tree of life (Genesis 3:22–24).

Yet even within the punishment for their sins, their forced exodus from the garden was an act of grace for their good. God kept them from living forever in their sinful state.

MIGRATION OF CAIN

The next account of migration is the result of Cain's act of murder. Part of his punishment was that he was to become "a fugitive and a wanderer on the earth" (Genesis 4:12). After Cain's conversation with God, Cain unfortunately "went away from the presence of the Lord and settled in the land of Nod, east of Eden" (Genesis 4:16).

At this point, it is important to compare these two accounts of migrations. Both were the result of sin. The rebellion in the garden and the murder of Abel had numerous terrible consequences, including a departure from the homeland. However, the responses of Adam and Eve and that of Cain following their migrations were radically different. The parents accepted the consequences of their acts and continued to remain with the Lord, giving credit to God for Seth (Genesis 4:25), whose line of descendents included the Messiah (Luke 3:23–38). Cain's response, on the other hand, was one of departure from God's presence.

MIGRATION AFTER THE FLOOD

Following the flood, the descendents of Noah multiplied and spread across the earth. Some of the descendents of Japheth migrated to the coastlands and "spread in their lands, each with his own language, by their clans, in their nations" (Genesis 10:5). Some of the descendents of Ham migrated to Egypt, Assyria, and Canaan (Genesis 10:6, 11, 15 19). The sons of Shem migrated to the "hill country of the east" (Genesis 10:30).

Before entering into the discussion of the events at Babel, Moses summarized the great migrations of peoples after the flood by noting, "These are the clans of the sons of Noah, according to their genealogies, in their nations, and from these the nations spread abroad on the earth after the flood" (Genesis 10:32).

MIGRATION AFTER BABEL

Since Genesis 10 records the presence of different languages (Genesis 10:5), we can assume that the Babel account of Genesis 11 occurred sometime before the events summarized in chapter 10. We read that the peoples of the earth migrated to the east, settled on a plain in Shinar, and all spoke one language (Genesis 11:1–2).

It is clear that they decided to deliberately disobey God's command to fill the earth, for they stated, "Let us make a name for ourselves, lest we be dispersed over the face of the whole earth" (Genesis 11:4). On the plain of Shinar the people ceased their migration pattern to satisfy their selfish cravings. They defiantly created a city and a tower as a monument to their abilities (Genesis 11:4).

Again, along with punishment for their sins, the grace of God is evident. Instead of allowing the people to continue for generation after generation in their disobedience, the Lord gave them different languages. They then dispersed across the earth according to their languages (Genesis 11:6–9). Over time this resulted in the establishment of tribes, villages, towns, cities, and nations.

ABRAHAM, ISAAC, AND JACOB

Like many of his day, Abram was a migrant. He and his extended family traveled east from Ur and settled in Haran (Genesis 11:31). It was here that the Lord called Abram to himself (Genesis 12:1; Acts 7:2–4) and urged him to continue his journey to Canaan, a land that God would reveal to him. There God promised that Abram's descendants would become a great nation so that "in [him] all the families of the earth" would be blessed (Genesis 12:3). For many years Abram migrated to different locations, including Egypt to escape a famine (Genesis 12:10), parting ways with Lot over available natural resources (Genesis 13:6–9), and sojourning in the land God promised to his descendents (Genesis 13:14–18).

It was during the time when God was making his covenant with Abram that he revealed another migration to come:

> Then the LORD said to Abram, "Know for certain that your offspring will be sojourners in a land that is not theirs and will be servants there, and they will be afflicted for four hundred years. But I will bring judgment on the nation that they serve, and afterward they shall come out with great possessions. As for you, you shall go to your fathers in peace; you shall be buried in a good old age. And they shall come back here in the fourth generation, for the iniquity of the Amorites is not yet complete." (Genesis 15:13–16)

What followed was Abram's great-grandchildren taking advantage of the slave trade and selling their brother Joseph into bondage. This resulted in the children of Jacob (Israel) migrating to Egypt in order to survive a famine; later generations then became slaves. Again, there is a juxtaposition of the consequences of the sinful acts of people with the sovereign grace of God. Jacob's sons attempted to harm their brother, but God worked through Joseph's forced migration to save the people who would eventually bring forth the Messiah. Also, God displayed his patience toward the Amorites of Canaan. For over four hundred years, he would be patient toward them, allowing them generations of time for their repentance. Then through a great diaspora from Egypt, he would use the sword of his people to bring about his judgment on the unrepentant Amorites.

Isaac also would experience life as a sojourner in another land. During his day, another famine came on the people. Isaac settled in

Gerar, for the Lord warned him not to travel into Egypt (Genesis 26:1–3). The Lord also instructed him to dwell in the land, for eventually he would receive this territory as a part of the ongoing process to bless the nations (Genesis 26:4). He was later told by the king of the Philistines to leave the area, so he settled in the valley of Gerar and eventually moved to Beersheba (Genesis 26:17, 23).

Isaac's son Jacob was also a man on the move throughout his life. Isaac directed him to go to Paddan-aram to find a wife (Genesis 28:2). On his way, as he camped for the night, he had a dream in which the Lord appeared to him. The Lord told Jacob that he would receive the land on which he was sleeping, that his offspring would travel abroad to the north, south, east, and west, and that through him and his offspring all the peoples of the earth would be blessed (Genesis 28:14–15). After many years in Paddam-aram, Jacob was told to return to the land of his fathers (Genesis 31:3).

Following his son Joseph's rise to power in Egypt, Jacob and his family migrated to Egypt and took up residence to be spared from a prolonged famine. The descendants of Jacob remained in Egypt for four hundred years before their mass exodus back to the Promised Land.

JOSEPH: MIGRATION THROUGH SLAVE TRADE

As mentioned above, Joseph is another example of the hand of the Lord at work through the wickedness of men. Through forced migration—the slave trade—Joseph was relocated to Egypt to serve Potiphar (Genesis 37). Though Joseph experienced numerous tragic events, the Lord was with him. Joseph rose to a position of great power and was able to save many people from starvation—including his extended family. His words to his brothers are a powerful testimony to the work of the Lord through a tragic migration: "And God sent me before you to preserve for you a remnant on earth, and to keep alive for you many survivors. So it was not you who sent me here, but God. . . . You meant evil against me, but God meant it for good, to bring it about that many people should be kept alive, as they are today" (Genesis 45:7–8; 50:20).

Even though Joseph was intimately connected to the people and culture of Egypt, he foretold a day when God would visit his people and have them migrate back to the land that he promised to Abraham, Isaac, and Jacob (Genesis 50:24).

FROM EXODUS TO THE PROMISED LAND

The greatest migration in the Old Testament is that of the departure of the descendants of Jacob from the bondage of Egypt's system of slavery. Following God's judgment by the ten plagues, the Egyptians allowed the Israelites to leave. But while camped near the border of the Promised Land, upon hearing of the report of the spies, the Israelites rebelled against God and entered into forty years of migration.

RUTH

There are numerous accounts of individual migrations peppered throughout the Old Testament. One such case that is critical to the outworking of God's plan of salvation in the world is related to Ruth. During a time of famine in Judah, Elimelech and Naomi migrated with their sons to Moab (Ruth 1:1–2). There the sons married Moabite women, one of whom was Ruth (Ruth 1:4), and later Elimelech and his sons died.

After hearing that "the Lord had visited his people and given them food," Naomi made preparations to return to Judah and planned on leaving her surviving daughters-in-law in Moab (Ruth 1:6–8). Although one of them did decide to remain in Moab, Ruth decided to go with Naomi and migrate to Bethlehem. Eventually, Ruth married Naomi's relative Boaz and gave birth to Obed, who would father Jesse, whose son was King David (Ruth 4:22). And it was through the line of Boaz and Ruth that Jesus would be born (Matthew 1:5, 16).

FROM ISRAEL TO ASSYRIA

As a result of Israel's continued rebellion against God, the nation of Assyria invaded their country and deported a large number of people in 722 BC. And while the captivity and relocation of God's people was a dark time in their history, the grace of God was still found in his judgment on their wickedness.

It was during this time in Israel's history that Isaiah provided the people with the prophecy of the birth of an eternal ruler whose "government shall be upon his shoulder, and his name shall be called Wonderful Counselor, Mighty God, Everlasting Father, Prince of Peace. Of the increase of his government and of peace there will be no end, on the throne of David and over his kingdom, to establish it and to uphold it with justice and with righteousness from this time forth and forevermore" (Isaiah 9:6–7).

And for those who were forced to migrate out of their Promised Land due to war, the Lord reminded them that his people would return to the land, and he would keep his promise to Abraham, Isaac, and Jacob:

> A remnant will return, the remnant of Jacob, to the mighty God. For though your people Israel be as the sand of the sea, only a remnant of them will return. Destruction is decreed, overflowing with righteousness. For the Lord GOD of hosts will make a full end, as decreed, in the midst of all the earth.
>
> Therefore thus says the Lord GOD of hosts: "O my people, who dwell in Zion, be not afraid of the Assyrians when they strike with the rod and lift up their staff against you as the Egyptians did. For in a very little while my fury will come to an end, and my anger will be directed to their destruction. And the LORD of hosts will wield against them a whip, as when he struck Midian at the rock of Oreb. And his staff will be over the sea, and he will lift it as he did in Egypt. And in that day

his burden will depart from your shoulder, and his yoke from your neck." (Isaiah 10:21–27)

FROM ISRAEL TO BABYLON

By 587 BC Babylon, the superpower of the region, invaded Jerusalem, forcing many of the people into captivity. Great destruction came upon the people and the land during these days. Jeremiah delivered a message to God's people that they would remain in Babylonian captivity for seventy years and were to make themselves as comfortable as possible while in exile. Even during these dark days, when it seemed that God was abandoning his people, Jeremiah delivered several messages of hope.

Jeremiah prophesied that "the days are coming, declares the LORD, when I will raise up for David a righteous Branch, and he shall reign as king and deal wisely, and shall execute justice and righteousness in the land. In his days Judah will be saved, and Israel will dwell securely" (Jeremiah 23:5–6). And while he told the people to prepare for seventy years of living as a diaspora, Jeremiah also spoke for the Lord when he said: "I will visit you, and I will fulfill to you my promise and bring you back to this place. For I know the plans I have for you, declares the LORD, plans for welfare and not for evil, to give you a future and a hope. . . . I will restore your fortunes and gather you from all the nations and all the places where I have driven you, declares the LORD, and I will bring you back to the place from which I sent you into exile" (Jeremiah 29:10–11, 14).

A remnant of the people of Israel would eventually migrate back to their land, but they would be a weakened nation under foreign domination. Yet in spite of the devastation of the years of war, exile, and Babylonian rule, the promises of God were fulfilled. About four hundred years would pass from the time of Malachi, the last prophet of the Old Testament, to the days of King Herod and the New Testament times.

CONCLUSION

The Old Testament is filled with examples of people and nations on the move. Some of these migrations were the result of sinful acts; others were responses to famine or war. Some migrations were made willingly, others by force. Yet in each move of the nations, God's hand was working out his plan of redemption and restoration in the world.

Early in the book of Genesis, we read that the divine mandate involved the filling of the earth. Such was only possible as people multiplied, moved, and developed communities across the planet. Shortly after this command was given, Adam and Eve were forced to migrate from the garden of Eden, and the movement of peoples began. And although sin had entered the world, the outworking of God's will was never thwarted.

And while the Old Testament begins with migration, Israel's history at the conclusion of the Old Testament writings also involves migration. While the nation of Babylon continued in unrepentant ways, even with the Israelites living among them, the Lord was raising up another superpower with which he would judge the Babylonians. The Persians became a mighty force of destruction, yet one the Lord would use to fulfill his promises. The writer of Second Chronicles recorded what would begin a migration of God's people back to Jerusalem to rebuild the temple:

> Now in the first year of Cyrus king of Persia, that the word of the LORD by the mouth of Jeremiah might be fulfilled, the LORD stirred up the spirit of Cyrus king of Persia, so that he made a proclamation throughout all his kingdom and also put it in writing: "Thus says Cyrus king of Persia, 'The LORD, the God of heaven, has given me all the kingdoms of the earth, and he has charged me to build him a house at Jerusalem, which is in Judah. Whoever is among you of all his people, may the LORD his God be with him. Let him go up'" (2 Chronicles 36:22–23).

As the Old Testament concludes, the divine hand is observed turning the heart of this king like a stream of water (Proverbs 21:1), in the outworking of the promise made in Eden that the seed of the woman would one day crush the head of the serpent (Genesis 3:15). The children of Abraham had indeed become as numerous as the stars in the sky and were migrating back to their land of promise. Yet this migration was the beginning of what would eventually lead to the fullness of time, when God would send forth his Son (Galatians 4:4), born of a woman—who would also quickly find herself forced to migrate to Egypt to save this promised Messiah.

Migration and Kingdom Expansion Part 2

PEOPLES ON THE MOVE

More than 40% of those who landed in Canada between 1982 and 2001 had a high degree of religiosity. Never before has Canada received such large concentrations of peoples from Asia, the Middle East, and Africa who practice Hinduism, Buddhism, Sikhism, and Islam. Although Muslims make up just over 2% of the population, they are the fastest-growing religious group in the country and expected to comprise almost 8% of the population by 2031.[1]

■　■　■

GENERATIONS AFTER THE REBUILDING of the city of Jerusalem, Greeks rose to become the world's superpower and spread Hellenism far and wide. By the time we encounter the characters of the New Testament, the Greeks had fallen to the Romans. Over the centuries some of the Jewish people had scattered abroad; however, many still lived in Israel. The Lord remained over the nations, continuing to work out his mission as time moved toward the day of the Lord and the restoration of creation.

Hellenism and Roman rule were the globalizing forces of New Testament times. Greek was the common language, and the construction of the Roman road system greatly enhanced and secured trade and mobility. The *pax Romana* (Roman peace through iron-fisted control) had ushered in a time of relative stability across that part of the world.

While many of the Jewish people had scattered across the Roman empire, crowds returned to Jerusalem for significant religious festivals. We observe the geographical and cultural range of the Diaspora Jews and the converts to Judaism on the day of Pentecost:

> Now there were dwelling in Jerusalem Jews, devout men from every nation under heaven. And at this sound the multitude came together, and they were bewildered, because each one was hearing them speak in his own language. And they were amazed and astonished, saying, "Are not all these who are speaking Galileans? And how is it that we hear, each of us in his own native language? Parthians and Medes and Elamites and residents of Mesopotamia, Judea and Cappadocia, Pontus and Asia, Phrygia and Pamphylia, Egypt and the parts of Libya belonging to Cyrene, and visitors from Rome, both Jews and proselytes, Cretans and Arabians—we hear them telling in our own tongues the mighty works of God." (Acts 2:5–11)

Those visiting Jerusalem from all of these nations would most likely have remained there for quite some time. As pilgrims to the holy city, they would have arrived to celebrate the Passover and remained through Pentecost (fifty days later). So at this moment in history, these followers of Judaism not only observed the fulfilling of the prophecy by Joel (Acts 2:16–17), but many also were the initial recipients of the outpouring of the Spirit as prophesied. The scattering of these pilgrims back to their homes across the Roman world was the beginning of a great dissemination of the gospel. Centuries of forced and voluntary migration of the Jewish people had set the stage for the making of disciples of all nations.

THE BIRTH OF JESUS

Paul wrote that in the fullness of time God sent his Son to be born (Galatians 4:4). Centuries of change, the rise and fall of governments, the development of cultures, economic shifts, and the movement of peoples helped set the stage for the incarnation. The fulfillment of Micah's prophecy of the birth of Jesus (Micah 5:2) involved Joseph and Mary departing Nazareth for Bethlehem to participate in the census declared by Caesar Augustus (Luke 2:1–7).

Immediately following the magi's departure from Bethlehem, the Lord commanded Joseph to flee to Egypt. While this migration was to fulfill Hosea's prophecy (Hosea 11:1; Matthew 2:15), it was a forced migration in response to Herod's infanticide. James K. Hoffmeier drew attention to this situation: "What is forgotten about this familiar story is that for a period of several years, Joseph, Mary, and Jesus were themselves refugees in Egypt. The Gospels pass over this segment of the life of Jesus in silence. We do not know under what circumstances they entered Egypt and where the Holy Family lived."[2]

Following Herod's death, Joseph, Mary, and Jesus migrated to Nazareth, thus fulfilling another prophecy (Matthew 2:23) related to the Messiah.

THE JERUSALEM PERSECUTION

Following the martyrdom of Stephen, a great persecution against the Jerusalem church erupted. The disciples scattered throughout the regions of Judea and Samaria, except the apostles (Acts 8:1). While this persecution resulted in the imprisonment of many men and women, the dispersion of the believers resulted in a continued dissemination of the gospel, fulfilling the expectation of Acts 1:8. The migrations of the believers out of the city resulted in a church being planted in Samaria, the gospel going into North Africa, and the planting of the church in Antioch—out of which Paul's missionary teams would be sent.

THE SAMARITANS

The Samaritans were not considered Jewish. As a result of the Assyrian invasions centuries before, many of the Israelites intermarried with the Assyrians. The result was a mixed race known as the Samaritans, despised by many Jews. Jesus initiated a great awakening in a Samaritan village (John 4), and later Philip evangelized in Samaria and many came to faith (Acts 8:5–8).

AN ETHIOPIAN

Following Philip's work in Samaria, he was led to the road that connected Jerusalem and Gaza. The Lord brought him to an Ethiopian who had been in Jerusalem worshiping and was returning home. After Philip encountered this man and explained to him a passage from the book of Isaiah, the Ethiopian believed and was baptized (Acts 8:26–39).

PHOENICIA, CYPRUS, AND ANTIOCH

The persecution following the death of Stephen resulted in the migration of believers into Phoenicia, Cyprus, and Antioch, and as they migrated, they preached the gospel (Acts 11:19). A church was birthed in Antioch with a great number of people (Acts 11:21). Later Barnabas and Paul would be instrumental in helping to strengthen this church and would be sent out as missionaries to plant other churches (Acts 13:1–3).

While the church in Antioch was very significant to Paul and his ministry, it is important to see the connection of forced migrations and global evangelization here. Though the diaspora of believers departing Jerusalem was not a pleasant matter, it resulted in a vast advancement of the gospel and the multiplication of churches. The gospel transformed many communities as the Word spread. As a result of the persecution, not only Samaritans but also Greeks in Antioch heard the truth (Acts 11:20). As Paul and his teams ventured out from the church in Antioch, they advanced the gospel and planted churches across the Roman empire. Paul wrote letters to many of these newly planted churches—letters that came to comprise a large portion of the New Testament.

PAUL'S MISSIONARY JOURNEYS

An examination of the life of Paul reveals that he was a man on the move. He was born in Tarsus in the region of Cilicia but raised and educated in Jerusalem (Acts 22:3). Near the end of the book of Acts, we read that he was taken to Rome and remained under house arrest while continuing to share the gospel (Acts 28:11–31).

Paul's ministry was to the Jew first and then to the Gentile (Romans 1:16). The practical outworking of this theology can be seen in the fact that when Paul found synagogues along his missionary routes, these would be the first places he engaged people with the gospel.

The missionary journeys reveal the wide range of the Jewish diaspora. For example, Acts records synagogues in Salamis (Acts 13:5), Pisidian Antioch (Acts 13:14), Iconium (Acts 14:1), Thessalonica (Acts 17:1), Berea (Acts 17:10), Corinth (Acts 18:7–8), and Ephesus (Acts 18:24–26).

Many Jews also were living in Italy and throughout Asia Minor. In Corinth Paul met Priscilla and Aquila and learned that this Jewish husband and wife had been forced to migrate from Rome when Emperor Claudius had expelled all the Jews from that area (Acts 18:2). Luke recorded that when Paul was in Ephesus, reasoning daily in the hall of Tyrannus, over the course of two years "all the residents of Asia heard the word of the Lord, both Jews and Greeks" (Acts 19:10).

ATHENS

Paul recognized that the centuries of global migrations since the days of Noah had not occurred by happenstance. They were not random moves of people based purely on economics, governmental decisions, war, famine, or persecution. Rather, God was sovereignly at work to bring the nations to himself. As mentioned in chapter 1, Paul's Mars Hill address in Athens reveals that God "made from one man every nation of mankind to live on all the face of the earth, having determined allotted periods and the boundaries of their dwelling place, that they should seek God, in the hope that they might feel their way toward him and find him. Yet he is actually not far from each one of us" (Acts 17:26–27).

And while God has allowed the locations of peoples to be established so that they may come to him, he has also determined that the means of this salvation is to come through the church preaching the good news. Paul recognized these matters and explained in his letter to the Romans that salvation is for both the Jew and the Gentile (Romans 3:29–30). Yet the only way for all the nations to hear the message of hope is for someone to go and share it with them (Romans 10:14–15). Paul would later write that he desired to travel to Spain to share this message, for he had shared it from Jerusalem all the way to Illyricum and fulfilled the ministry in that area (Romans 15:19, 24).

BELIEVERS DURING THE DISPERSION

Kingdom citizens are all sojourners in this world. Chapter 11 of the book of Hebrews offers examples of people of faith. Evident in this long list of the faithful is the idea that these believers lived their lives as journeys to a better place. Followers of Jesus walk by faith, not for the comfort of this world but for a city yet to be seen. Abraham is one example here: "By faith Abraham obeyed when he was called to go out to a place that he was to receive as an inheritance. And he went out, not knowing where he was going. By faith he went to live in the land of promise, as in a foreign land, living in tents with Isaac and Jacob, heirs with him of the same

promise. For he was looking forward to the city that has founda-
tions, whose designer and builder is God" (Hebrews 11:8–10).
The author of Hebrews continued his list of individuals, noting:

> These all died in faith, not having received the things promised,
> but having seen them and greeted them from afar, and having
> acknowledged that they were strangers and exiles on the earth.
> For people who speak thus make it clear that they are seeking
> a homeland. If they had been thinking of that land from which
> they had gone out, they would have had opportunity to return.
> But as it is, they desire a better country, that is, a heavenly one.
> Therefore God is not ashamed to be called their God, for he
> has prepared for them a city. (Hebrews 11:13–16)

The notion that the citizenship of the followers of Jesus is not in
this world is brought up again in other epistles. James addressed
his letter to "the twelve tribes in the Dispersion" (James 1:1). This
Jewish language would have resonated with James's readers, especially those who were Jewish by race. His letter still reminds those
scattered throughout the world how to live during their times of
trials (James 1:2).

In his first letter, Peter wrote to "those who are elect exiles of the
Dispersion in Pontus, Galatia, Cappadocia, Asia, and Bithynia" (1
Peter 1:1). These followers of Jesus also were undergoing many trials.
Peter's writing is filled with Old Testament imagery. He reminded
his readers that even though they were not living in the Promised
Land, as exiles sojourning throughout this world (1 Peter 2:11) they
were nevertheless a "chosen race, a royal priesthood, a holy nation, a
people for his own possession" so that they could "proclaim the ex-
cellencies of him who called you out of darkness into his marvelous
light" (1 Peter 2:9). God calls believers to be holy in Christ, as he is
holy (1 Peter 1:15).

CONCLUSION

In these two last chapters, we have examined several passages throughout the Scriptures related to migration and God's outworking of salvation history. Jehu J. Hanciles's observation sums up well what I have attempted to describe in these chapters:

Crucially, the interface between human mobility and divine purposes in the biblical story is unmistakable and compelling. The inextricable link between migrant movement and the *missio dei* (the mission of God) arguably confirms the historicity of many events. It is also strongly paradigmatic of the biblical God's intimate involvement in human affairs. In other words, to claim that the God of the Bible is a God of mission is to accept that he makes himself known to human beings through ordinary, culturally conditioned experiences. And, as already noted, few experiences are more basic to the human condition than migration. Significantly, migration and exile form bookends (of sorts) to the biblical record: the earliest chapters record the expulsion of Adam and Eve from the Garden of Eden (Gen 3:23), and the last book contains the magnificent vision of the apostle John, who is exiled on the island of Patmos (Rev 1:9).[3]

Migration and the West, 1500–2010

PEOPLES ON THE MOVE

While Boston's Chinatown is the second largest on the East Coast, following New York's, if you travel twenty-five minutes south of downtown Boston, you will encounter twice as many Chinese Americans as are living downtown. In the 1990s Quincy, Massachusetts's Asian population increased by 144%, with two-thirds of those being Chinese. The Vietnamese and South Asian Indians comprise the second- and third-largest Asian subgroups, respectively. A conservative estimate is that 17% of Quincy's population is Asian.[1]

■   ■   ■

THE PRESENT AND FUTURE ARE SHAPED and influenced by the past. A strong connection exists between the movement of the 3 percent of the world's peoples to outside their countries of birth and the histories of those peoples. In order to get a better understanding of the present realities of such migrations, this chapter will provide a brief survey of the history of migration to the West. While entire books have been written on the topic of the history of human migrations,[2] this chapter will focus on a time period beginning in 1500 with European colonial expansion and ending in 2010. I have organized this chapter according to the following epochs:

- 1500–1850: European Colonialism and African-Slave-Trade Era
- 1850–1945: Industrial Era
- 1945–Present: Postindustrial Global Migrations Era

1500–1850: EUROPEAN COLONIALISM AND AFRICAN-SLAVE-TRADE ERA

While peoples have always been on the move, European exploration and trade in the late fifteenth and early sixteenth centuries introduced a new measure of mobility, economic and territorial expansion, and how people thought about the world. In an attempt to find better trade routes to the East, European explorers traveled west, running into what is now called North and South America. Soon explorers from Spain, Portugal, France, and England sought to stake their claims in these regions of the world. By conquest and settlement they obtained the coveted territories from native populations who had likely migrated out of Asia and settled in North and South America centuries before the Europeans arrived.

From the seventeenth to the nineteenth centuries, European nations established their colonies across the world. The European perspective was that there was little value in the cultures of the peoples of the world; European ways were "civilized" and should be taught to non-Europeans. The notion of "Christianize and civilize" was woven throughout many missionary strategies. European colonists migrated to what would become the United States and Canada, South America, Africa, Australia, and New Zealand.[3] The establishment of European control in these and other areas of the world would later be instrumental in the migrations of peoples to Western Europe. As European governments returned power to the nationals in the lands that had been under their control, many peoples migrated to England, France, and Spain looking for a better quality of life.

It was during this period that the rise in the Atlantic slave trade developed, using Africans as a commodity. While the European trade began in the 1440s to provide labor for European colonies in Central and South America and the Caribbean, over the four hundred years of its existence (sixteenth through nineteenth centuries), thirteen million Africans were removed from their homeland and shipped against their will to the West.[4]

During this epoch many Europeans became indentured servants in order to migrate to the New World in search of a better way of life. By 1776 at least 10 percent of the population of the thirteen colonies was Irish. Kirby Miller and Paul Wagner noted that of the Irish immigrants of the eighteenth through the twentieth centuries, seven million crossed the Atlantic to their new homeland. Today forty million Americans can trace all or part of their ancestry to those seven million migrants.[5] Peoples from other countries came to America as well. From 1800 to 1860, according to Castles and Miller, 66 percent of the migrants to the United States were British and 22 percent were German.[6] Also, the Chinese started arriving in the late 1840s, about the same time as the Germans and Irish.[7]

1850–1945: INDUSTRIAL ERA

In less than 150 years following 1750, over thirty-five million Europeans departed their homelands. From Ireland four and a half million departed for the West. Over four million left Great Britain. Six million left the heart of the continent, from what would later become the German Empire. Two million Scandinavians and approximately five million Italians emigrated. Eight million Poles, Jews, Hungarians, Bohemians, Slovaks, Ukrainians, and Ruthenians moved to the West. Three million departed from the Balkans and Asian Minor (Greeks, Macedonians, Croatians, Albanians, Syrians, and Armenians).[8]

As word began to spread regarding the promise of jobs in the United States, Europeans began to emigrate in massive numbers.

From 1850 to 1914 most of the migrants were from Ireland, Italy, Spain, and Eastern Europe.[9] Between 1850 and 1920 Europeans migrated to Canada, the United States, Mexico, and South America.[10]

W. M. Spellman noted that from 1800 to 1914, some fifty million migrants settled in five countries: Argentina, Australia, New Zealand, Canada, and the United States, with the latter receiving thirty-three million people. By the time of the First World War, 21 percent of ethnic Europeans were living outside their homelands, compared to 4 percent in 1800.[11]

Canada began receiving migrants from China, Japan, and India in the late nineteenth century. Between 1895 and 1914 many Southern and Eastern Europeans arrived. While British settlers and convict transportation helped build the Australian population in this period, laborers also came from China, India, and the South Pacific Islands. After the settling of British migrants in New Zealand in the 1830s, Chinese workers were recruited to work in the 1860s and following.[12] France experienced an influx of over two million people between the 1880s and the 1930s, mostly from Belgium, Italy, and Poland. Spaniards fleeing civil war in the 1930s also added to this group.[13]

Until the 1880s illegal entry into the United States did not exist. In 1882 the Chinese Exclusion Act was passed, limiting the numbers of Chinese laborers and families who could immigrate to the United States.[14] Later the Immigration Act of 1917 required a literacy test for immigrants and allowed for a greater exclusion of potential immigrants based on physical, mental, moral, and other standards. The limitations from these two acts were not removed until the 1960s.[15]

Following World War I, immigration patterns and policies changed. The somewhat open policies of the eighteenth and nineteenth centuries faded, and the twentieth century saw more challenges for international migrants, including the requirement of extensive documentation.[16]

1945–PRESENT: POSTINDUSTRIAL
GLOBAL MIGRATIONS ERA

The Second World War led to the rise of a new challenge in the area of migration—the refugee. Although there have always been people fleeing their homelands, in the twentieth and twenty-first centuries their numbers were of such a magnitude that a body of international laws was developed regarding how nations should respond. The United Nations Refugee Agency was developed after WWII to assist Europeans who had been affected by the conflict. By 1950 the United Nations had established the United Nations High Commissioner for Refugees (UNHCR). The original plan was for this office to exist for three years, complete its task, and disband; however, refugee crises around the world continued to escalate, and sixty years later the UNHCR is still active.[17] The 1951 Geneva Convention relating to the status of refugees developed the legal documents that, to this day, define who refugees are, their rights, and the obligations of the countries that receive them.[18]

Regular commercial air travel and advancements in telecommunications have assisted in the growth and speed of migrations. Other contributors to the rise in migrations during this epoch include the collapse of the Soviet empire, famine, wars, and ethnic cleansing. Such acceleration in the numbers of peoples migrating led Castles and Miller to label our present period the Age of Migration.[19] While the number of international migrants (214 million, 3 percent of the world's population) may not appear to be a large proportion, James Hollifield reminds us that "the perception is that international migration is rising at an exponential rate and that it is a permanent feature of the global economy."[20] It should also be remembered that if the number of international migrants represented a single country's population, it would be the fifth-largest nation in the world.

James V. Spickard and Afe Adogame have noted that our highly interconnected globe has influenced migration in a new way in addition to the numbers of those migrating. "It is not just the number of people on the go, nor their reasons, though these matter," they observe. "It is the fact that they are going everywhere at once, in all directions, even as they remain connected with all the places that they have been."[21]

Since the middle of the twentieth century, the movement of peoples has no longer been primarily from Europe to North America. Across the world people are migrating from countries with weaker economies to those with stronger economies, with the latter not being limited to the West. However, many of the present trends are movements from the Majority World to the West, or to use another set of terms, from the Global South to the Global North. Countries such as the United States, Canada, those in Western Europe, Australia, and New Zealand receive large numbers of international migrants.

According to Castles and Miller, there were common features of the Western migrations occurring from 1945 to 1973. First, most of the migrants were pushed from their countries out of the need for work and pulled to those countries actively recruiting and extending worker invitations. Such economic matters were strong motivators for moving. Second, a growing ethnic and cultural diversity developed over time. In the beginning most migrants were from European countries. However, more and more peoples from Asia, Africa, and Latin America started to migrate in search of jobs.[22]

Many countries that had long-established colonies in the world experienced a large influx of migrants as workers from their former colonies. For example, by 1970 France received over 600,000 Algerians, 140,000 Moroccans, and 90,000 Tunisians. Other workers were coming from Senegal, Mali, and Mauritania.[23]

Changes in the United States immigration policy in 1965 resulted in a rapid rise in the number of migrants from Asia and Latin America. Canada also experienced changes in its migration policy in the 1960s, leading to an increase in the number of non-European arrivals.

By the early twenty-first century, three of the larger foreign communities in the Netherlands were from Surinam, Indonesia, and

Turkey, with approximately 200,000 people from each country. The Moroccan presence was 150,000 people. In Spain the Moroccans numbered 310,000. While the United Kingdom's Indian population was at one million; African peoples from South Africa, Kenya, and Nigeria numbered about 100,000. Italy received 200,000 migrants from the former Yugoslavia and 155,000 Moroccans. In Belgium the main migrant communities were from Morocco (100,000), Turkey (70,000), and the Democratic Republic of Congo (40,000). Portugal experienced many migrations from former colonies such as Angola (175,000), Mozambique (75,000), Brazil (50,000), Cape Verde (45,000), and Guinea Bissau (20,000). In France migrants from Algeria, Morocco, and Tunisia represented 2.3 million people, Turkey 180,000, Vietnam 115,000, Senegal 80,000, Madagascar 70,000, Côte d'Ivoire 45,000, and Mali 40,000.[24]

Today the migrations of Majority World peoples to the Western world are commonplace. Billions in remittances are sent home to relatives and communities every year, with many Majority World countries heavily dependent on such monetary returns. Social networks and support systems are established in many parts of the West, opening doors for others to migrate and keeping doors open for relatives to return to their country of birth. Table 6.1 offers a glance at the approximate numbers of international migrants in the West as of 2010.

Table 6.1 International Migrants in Western Countries, 2010 Estimates[25]

Country	Estimated Number of International Migrants, 2010	International Migrants as a Percentage of the Population, 2010
Australia	4,711,490	21.9
Austria	1,310,218	15.6
Belgium	974,849	9.1
Canada	7,202,340	21.3
Denmark	483,714	8.8
Finland	225,646	4.2
France	6,684,842	10.7

Country	Estimated Number of International Migrants, 2010	International Migrants as a Percentage of the Population, 2010
Germany	10,758,061	13.1
Greenland	5,823	10.2
Hungary	368,076	3.7
Iceland	37,223	11.3
Ireland	898,630	19.6
Italy	4,463,413	7.4
Liechtenstein	12,538	34.6
Luxembourg	173,232	35.2
Netherlands	1,752,869	10.5
New Zealand	962,072	22.4
Norway	485,444	10.0
Portugal	918,626	8.6
South Africa	1,862,889	3.7
Spain	6,377,524	14.1
Sweden	1,306,020	14.1
Switzerland	1,762,797	23.2
United Kingdom	6,451,711	10.4
United States	42,813,281	13.5

CONCLUSION

The movement of peoples has been an amazing phenomenon across the last five hundred years. Whether people migrate due to wicked acts such as slave trade or to war or in an attempt to improve their way of life, the reality is that the peoples of the world are forever changed as a result of such movements.

The age of migration continues, and with such movements come great challenges. We simply need to watch the daily news to observe this. Whether it is the French government working to expel the thousands of Roma within its borders, the German government telling its Turkish citizens they must learn to speak German, the Australian government welcoming migrants but declaring that they must not expect Australians to give up their freedoms to make them feel welcome, the United States government wrestling with the ten million unauthorized migrants living within its borders, or the concerns of Italy's leaders at the arrival of thousands of Tunisian refugees, we are constantly being reminded that the peoples of this world are on the move.

Are we as followers of Jesus prepared for such wonderful opportunities to serve and share the only hope for abundant and eternal life? For the most part, I believe the church has neglected numerous similar opportunities in epochs past. Now we live in a time of unprecedented movement, and these are days of grand opportunity. The peoples of the world are now living next door to us. May we recognize the sovereign hand of the Lord who has moved them and join in his mission, that they may know him and make him known.

Students on the Move

PEOPLES ON THE MOVE

In 2001 it was estimated that ten thousand Gujarati Hindus settled in France, many coming as refugees from Uganda. In Paris fifty to sixty thousand Hindu Tamil refugees found asylum and established temples.[1]

Recently, Helsinki's eastern neighborhood Itäkeskus and other nearby communities have experienced a growth in the number of foreign-born residents. More than one-fifth of the population have foreign backgrounds, with their numbers increasing by about 1 percent per year.[2]

The Guatemalan community has been experiencing rapid growth in Brooklyn, New York. In 2005 there were 4,500 living in the community. By 2008 that number had risen to 12,000.[3]

■　■　■

As a university student, I was very involved in one of the Christian organizations on our campus. One night each week several of us would meet for prayer and then go to the dorms and apartments on campus to share Jesus with students who were interested in such discussions. I remember on one particular evening knocking on the door of an apartment and being greeted by a bleary-eyed student from the former Soviet Union. His apartment was dark, and his hair was disheveled; we obviously had awakened him. After spending a moment greeting him and apologizing for intruding on his rest, we found out that he was thankful for our intrusion. "I am glad you came by. My alarm did not go off, and I overslept for a meeting."

But he did not appear to be in a hurry. After he found out that we were followers of Jesus, he was interested in talking. "I am interested in finding out more. In my country we were taught atheism for many years. It is hard for me to believe. However, I do believe God sent you here to knock on my door and wake me for my meeting." After a few moments of talking with him about Jesus and leaving some material for him to read, we left, with him continuing to thank us for knocking on his door.

Here was an international student—who for most of his life was an atheist—now saying that he believed God cared enough about him to send Christians to wake him from his sleep. As we departed, we prayed that his awakening would be more than physical.

On another occasion during my collegiate years, I was scheduled to lead a training session in personal evangelism. While I knew most of the students who were present, I did not know the female Chinese student who showed up. Minutes before the session started, one of the girls in the group met me by the photocopier and informed me that she had been talking with the student and discovered that she was not a follower of Jesus. She had been in our building one night attending an event for international students, had seen some free pins we were giving away, and had thought she had to sign up for the event to take one. Now, here she was attending a training session on sharing one's faith, and she was not a believer. The Lord moves people in unusual ways!

The first session was "What Is the Gospel?" Needless to say, I explained it in a way that an unbeliever could grasp this great truth. I remember that just before the break, in broken English, the girl told the small group, "I am not a follower of Jesus. But this is a message I need to consider."

A visit to a random apartment, an alarm clock that did not work—and the movement of a Russian student to Central Kentucky. A free evangelistic button, a cultural misunderstanding—and the movement of a Chinese student across the world. All part of the gospel reaching into the lives of individuals who decided to study in the United States.

Over the years I have found that, like the students in these two stories, most international students are very open to discussing matters related to the gospel. While some may not be quick to repent and place faith in Jesus, they are willing to hear about such truth.

While taking a graduate course at the University of Louisville, I was paired with a student from India to work on a project together. We were assigned a social-research activity that had to be completed at one of the local malls. Since he did not have a car, I agreed to pick him up and take him home. As we traveled the local highway, I asked him questions about the South Asian Indian community in the city. After hearing of his interest in tea, soccer, and cricket, he finally shared his interest in American movies. "We watch a lot of movies. Sometimes we are bored. So we rent movies." I asked him what he had recently watched, knowing *The Passion of the Christ* had just been released on DVD. It did not take long before he stated that he and several men in his apartment complex had seen the film.

"What did you think about that movie?" I inquired.

"Oh, it was so bad what they did to that man."

Over the next few minutes, he shared with me portions from the film, probably not realizing that this was the gospel message from the Bible. I was able to use this opportunity to talk about who Jesus is, why he was killed and arose, and how we should respond. While this student was Hindu, he was extremely open to talking about Jesus, the Bible, and my experience.

In this chapter and much of the literature addressing international students, the focus is on students enrolled in higher education. But when we are thinking of reaching out to foreign students, we must include all levels of education—high school and vocational training as well as undergraduate and graduate studies.

NUMBERS OF STUDENTS ON THE MOVE

It was estimated in the year 2000 that there were 1.7 million international students at university or tertiary-level institutions.[4] By 2008 approximately 3 million students were enrolled in tertiary educational institutions outside of their countries of origin.[5] During that year Australia, Canada, France, South Africa, and the United Kingdom hosted 32 percent of the world's international students.[6] It is expected that the numbers of students studying outside their countries of birth will continue to increase.

One factor involved in this movement of students is that many member countries of the Organization for Economic Cooperation and Development (OECD) have taken the initiative not only to recruit students but also to make study at their institutions more appealing.[7] Some schools reduce costs related to studying abroad, offer English-language instruction, accept the transfer of student credits, and allow students to work part time.[8] OECD countries receive about 84% of all students studying abroad.[9] While the data are limited, the estimated stay rates for students who remain in the host country for work or other reasons and do not immediately return home vary between 15 and 35%, with an average of 21%.[10]

And while a considerable number of students remain in developed countries following graduation, many countries are working diligently to draw their people back home. According to Stephen Castles and Mark J. Miller, "Often Asian countries are seeking to lure back their own diasporas—the professionals and students who left in the past when there were few opportunities at home. Taiwan has been especially successful in maintaining contacts with expatriates and drawing them back as industrialization progressed, . . . and other countries are now trying to follow this example. The Chinese diaspora has been a crucial source of capital and expertise in the Chinese economic takeoff."[11]

Whether these students remain or return, there are great opportunities for gospel advancement with students. If they enter the workforce in their host countries, our relationships with them can continue. If they return immediately following the completion of their studies, our relationships can continue long distance. Technology and travel have made the development of long distance relationships possible.

WHO IS STUDYING IN THE WEST?

The United States, the United Kingdom, Germany, France, and Australia are the main destination countries for international students.[12] About 62 percent of the world's students studying outside of their homelands are studying in North America and Western Europe.

Table 7.1 Percentage of Students by Region Studying in North America and Western Europe, 2008[13]

Region	Number of Students Studying Abroad	Percentage Studying in North America and Western Europe
World	2,965,840	62.1%
Arab States	206,549	68.6%
Central/Eastern Europe	330,563	63.1%
Central Asia	96,314	17.3%
East Asia/Pacific	846,618	54.9%
Latin America/Caribbean	177,995	73.7%
South and West Asia	275,840	70.7%
Sub-Saharan Africa	223,181	65.1%

United States. Many students desire to study at colleges and universities in the United States. With all of its shortcomings, the quality of this education is still coveted throughout the world. Presently, 40% of doctoral degrees in science and engineering and 65% of those in computer science are granted to foreign students.[14] In the

2010-2011 academic year, the United States hosted 723,277 international students, with 214,490 new international students enrolling for the first time. The number of students from China increased by 23.5% from 2009-2010 to 2010-2011. During the same period, the number of students from Saudi Arabia increased by 43.6%, Iran by 18.9%, and Vietnam by 13.5%. Of the international students in the United States, 54% were from China, India, South Korea, Canada, and Taiwan in the 2010-2011 academic year.[15] Table 7.2 below offers a perspective of the top places of origin for international students studying in the United States from 2010 to 2011.

Table 7.2 Top Places of Origin for International Students in the US, 2010-2011.[16]

Rank	Country	2010-2011	Percentage of Total
	World Total	723,277	100
1	China	157,558	21.8
2	India	103,895	14.4
3	South Korea	73,351	10.1
4	Canada	27,546	3.8
5	Taiwan	24,818	3.4
6	Saudi Arabia	22,704	3.1
7	Japan	21,290	2.9
8	Vietnam	14,888	2.1
9	Mexico	13,713	1.9
10	Turkey	12,184	1.7
11	Nepal	10,301	1.4
12	Germany	9,458	1.3
13	United Kingdom	8,947	1.2
14	Brazil	8,777	1.2
15	Thailand	8,236	1.1
16	Hong Kong	8,136	1.1
17	France	8,098	1.1
18	Nigeria	7,148	1.0
19	Indonesia	6,942	1.0
20	Malaysia	6,735	0.9
21	Colombia	6,456	0.9
22	Iran	5,626	0.8
23	Venezuela	5,491	0.8
24	Pakistan	5,045	0.7
25	Russia	4,692	0.6

Canada. There were 79,500 international students studying in Canada in 2008. The country has been attempting to retain such students through extensions to its work-permit programs.[17]

United Kingdom. A study in higher education trends found that international students increased in the United Kingdom by 48 percent from 2000 to 2006, with 19,385 students coming from China. In the 2007-2008 period of time, 229,640 students came to the United Kingdom from outside the European Union.[18]

Austria. The number of international students in Austria has been increasing at a rapid rate. In 2005 there were 3,200 such students, but by 2008 an estimated 8,500 existed. This is almost a three-fold increase.[19]

France. From 2000 to 2005 the number of international students in France increased by one hundred thousand.[20] The annual number of international students was 49,750 in 2008. The main countries of origin were China, Morocco, Algeria, Tunisia, and the United States.[21]

Finland. One of the primary objectives of the Ministry of Education is to increase the number of international students studying in Finland. In 2008 authorities made decisions on 4,917 student-residence permit applications, a 21 percent increase over the previous year. It is expected that the number of applications from Africa will increase.[22]

Denmark. The number of international students in Denmark increased to 7,400 by 2008. This was a 76 percent increase over the year 2000.[23]

Sweden. The growth in the number of international students in Sweden has held constant, with an annual 14% rate since 1997. By 2007 the rate increased to 22% (8,900 students). In 2009 the numbers increased to 13,500.[24]

The following table shows the numbers of international students studying in selected European countries in 2008.

Table 7.3 International Students in Select European Countries, 2008[25]

Country	Number of International Students
Germany	58,400
Italy	37,200
Netherlands	13,500
Norway	5,900
Portugal	5,000
Spain	41,900
Switzerland	11,000

New Zealand. In 2008-2009 there were 73,926 international students approved to study in New Zeland. This was a 6 percent increase from the previous calendar year. Many of these students came from India.[26]

Australia. From 2000 to 2005 the number of international students in Australia increased by eighty-five thousand.[27] By 2007 they were hosting 7.6 percent of the world's mobile students.[28] Between 2003 and 2008 the number of students from China and India doubled, and the number from Vietnam tripled.[29] In 2010-2011, 464,955 students with visas arrived. The largest numbers came from the following countries: China (129,145, excludes Hong Kong, Macau, and Taiwan), India (34,742), Malaysia (31,934), Korea (21,015), and Indonesia (20,081).[30]

THE MOST INFLUENTIAL PEOPLE IN THE WORLD

Students in any country are among the most influential people in the world. They are tomorrow's (and oftentimes today's) leaders in politics, business, medicine, the arts, science, technology, and education. Students able to study in the West represent the best and the brightest of their home countries.

If we are to take the Great Commission seriously, we must recognize the enormous potential for the advancement of the gospel through students. In many countries, our Lord has used students to be significant contributors to great awakenings. Students are highly mobile, flexible, impressionable, progressive, often receptive, and generally deeply committed to the things of the Lord when they come to experience his grace. If the church is to reach the world, it must reach students.

CONCLUSION

Numerous stories abound revealing the impact of international students returning home with the gospel. Consider the following stories:

- **A migrant in Australia** shared a sermon tape with her parents back home in Hong Kong. After listening to the tape, the father became a Christian.

- **"An influential, staunch Muslim family** from a Middle Eastern country sent their son to study in India. The young man met us and asked for medical help for a long-standing physical problem. Because he had tried other treatments, all to no avail, we did not know what to do except to look to God. With much hesitation, we prayed over him. For three nights in succession, Jesus revealed himself in a dream. The ailment disappeared at once. The young man believed in Jesus and was baptized. Because he faced severe persecution in his home country, he is a church planter in another Middle Eastern country."[31]

- **Woodland Park Baptist Church** in Hammond, Louisiana, has seen students come to faith in Christ and return home to begin Bible studies. Dana Chastang, the director of international student ministry with the church, noted, "This is not something that happens quickly. It takes a lot of patience and time."[32]

- **Carol Pipes** shared the story of Nadeem Qazi's conversion experience as a student who returned to his people as a church planter:

  At the age of 25, Qazi left Pakistan to pursue a Ph.D. in Europe. He met a group of Christian students in Denmark who told him about a God of love who supplies all our needs. He heard this message at a time in his life when he felt utterly hopeless. Qazi gave his life to Christ.

Though his family said he was dead to them and never to return home, Qazi eventually returned to Pakistan to share the gospel and plant churches among his people. Several years later, the Pakistani government warned him to leave the country because his life was in danger. After migrating to Toronto, he now finds himself ministering among Hindu, Sikh, and Muslim groups, and leading a Bible study that meets in the home of a Sikh family who recently came to faith in Jesus.[33]

- **Bakht Singh** was a Sikh from northern India who came to Canada to study engineering. A Christian couple befriended him, witnessed to him, and gave him a Bible. Through these relationships Singh decided to follow Jesus. He later returned home as an engineer and church planter. Through his ministry, over seven hundred churches were planted in India, Pakistan, Sri Lanka, and Nepal.[34]

Refugees on the Move

PEOPLES ON THE MOVE

Beginning in 1975 about eighty to one hundred thousand Surinamese Hindustanis settled in the Netherlands. By 2001 about four thousand Tamil Hindu refugees from Sri Lanka found asylum there. It was estimated at the beginning of the twenty-first century that 2,900 Hindus were among the 3,500 Indian citizens living in the Netherlands.[1]

As of 2001, peoples with a Muslim cultural background residing in the Netherlands were comprised of several different people groups. They came from Turkey (241,000), Morocco (196,000), and Surinam (152,000, with about 50,000 being Muslim). Smaller groups came from Indonesia, the Molucca Islands, Pakistan, and Tunisia. Those with a shorter history in the Netherlands are refugees from Somalia, Iraq, Iran, and the former Yugoslavia.[2]

■ ■ ■

THE HEADLINE WOULD CATCH MOST PEOPLE'S ATTENTION: "First of 60,000 Refugees from Bhutan Arrive in U.S." It introduced an article that described a massive relocation of people from the other side of the world. Over the past seventeen years, 107,000 Bhutanese refugees, who are ethnically Nepali, have been living in seven United Nations camps in southeastern Nepal. The US government agreed to receive sixty thousand, with Australia, Canada, Norway,

Netherlands, New Zealand, and Denmark offering to resettle ten thousand each.[3] For centuries peoples have unfortunately had to flee their homes to avoid injury, death, persecution, and war. The Bhutanese are another people with another tragic story.

Not only do refugees face the challenges of leaving home, they also have numerous challenges facing them when they arrive at a safe destination. Take the Somali, for example. Columbus, Ohio, is home to the nation's second-largest Somali community (Minneapolis being number one). Many of the Somalis arrived as refugees; some had originally settled in Minnesota and Virginia. The local media has estimated the Somali population in Columbus at forty thousand and approximately 50 percent of the population at under age twenty-three. While this Little Somalia is also home to hundreds of Somali-run businesses, many people are having a very difficult time adjusting to the unfamiliar context.[4]

Many arrive without any knowledge of the English language. Few have any job skills for the market in Columbus. Public housing for many refugees is often crowded. Peoples of other ethnicities in the community do not understand the cultures of the refugees (and the opposite is true as well), leading to tensions and crime. Religious and dietary differences exist. Public schools have a difficult time absorbing the population increases and challenges refugee children bring to the classroom. The following quote provides a glimpse into the massive social disruption refugees experience:

> Refugees can no longer be understood merely as people who once had a static traditional culture that has been temporarily disrupted. The environments of refugees were usually unstable for a long time before the period of dislocation, and cross-border refugees may have already undergone a period of in-country displacement. Refugees must constantly re-create and redefine themselves—legally, culturally, and materially—as their set-

tings change. They are called on to create new structures in unfamiliar settings fairly quickly, submit to the authoritarian humanitarianism of camps overseen by bureaucrats, or adapt to asylum countries where they may be resented or hated.[5]

But the church can reach out and minister to those undergoing such transitions—that is, of course, if we know who the people are and where they are moving.

THE CENTURY OF THE REFUGEE

The twentieth century was the century of the refugee. Not only did the world witness the international development of a set of protocols for how nations should relate to those seeking asylum, but it was during this century that the world witnessed an enormous increase in their numbers.

The wake of World War II was the catalyst that led to the development of the office of the United Nations High Commissioner for Refugees (UNHCR). While the original plan was for the office to exist for three years to assist displaced Europeans, the refugee crises of the world continued to increase; and so the office continues today. In its first year, the annual budget was the equivalent of $300,000 (USD); it now exceeds $2 billion (USD). As of this writing, the UNHCR deals with 34.4 million people of concern.[6]

The official UNHCR definition of a refugee is someone who has "well-founded fear of being persecuted for reasons of race, religion, nationality, membership of a particular social group or political opinion, is outside the country of his nationality and is unable or, owing to such fear, is unwilling to avail himself of the protection of that country; or who, not having a nationality and being outside the country of his former habitual residence as a result of such events, is unable or, owing to such fear, is unwilling to return to it."[7]

Of all of the people on the move, these are the most in need of compassion, assistance, and good news. Some are internally displaced within their own countries; others have fled their homes, properties, and sometimes their families to find asylum in safer countries.[8] The majority seek refuge within their homeland or a nearby country. Others attempt to move far from home. Those who flee great distances often have no language or job skills once they arrive at their destinations. They come from Majority World countries, only to find themselves in extremely unfamiliar social environments. Some will leave home and have to live for years in refugee camps, waiting to be relocated to another country. Those seeking refugee status experience enormous social, psychological, and emotional upheaval and often physical harm. The severe plight of those seeking refugee status offers a great opportunity for the church to take action and help the helpless.

THE GLOBAL REALITIES

The UNHCR noted that in 2010

- There were 10.55 million refugees

- There were 14.7 million internally displaced persons

- There were 837,500 asylum seekers

- Pakistan hosted the largest number of refugees (1.9 million), followed by the Islamic Republic of Iran (1.1 million), the Syrian Arab Republic (1 million), and Germany (594,000)

- Developing countries hosted 80% of the global refugee population

- Asia had 54% of the global refugee population, followed by Africa (23%), Europe (15%), and North America (4%)

- Afghanistan was the largest country of origin of refugees (3 million), followed by Iraq (1.7 million), Somalia (770,000), the Democratic Republic of the Congo (477,000), and Myanmar (416,000)

- Among the top Western refugee hosting countries, Germany hosted 594,300 refugees, followed by the United States (264,600) and the United Kingdom (238,100)

- The countries resettling the most refugees were the United States (71,400), Canada (12,100), Australia (8,500), Sweden (1,800), and Norway (1,100)

- The most sought-after destination for asylum-seekers was South Africa, followed by the United States, France, Germany, and Sweden

- Refugees and asylum-seekers were more often established in urban contexts

- Among refugees and people in refugee-like situations, children comprised 44% of the population[9]

PROTRACTED REFUGEE SITUATIONS

The UNHCR provides different designations for the world's refugees, depending on their differing situations. One important category that we need to understand is that of the *protracted refugee*. This situation is defined as one "in which 25,000 or more refugees of the same nationality have been in exile for five years or longer in any given asylum country." When this definition is applied to the global refugee population, it is estimated that 5.5 million refugees were in a protracted situation in 2009.[10]

The following table displays the countries that hosted the largest numbers of refugees as of the end of 2010.

Table 8.1 Major Refugee-Hosting Countries[11]

Country	Number of Refugees
Pakistan	1,900,621
Islamic Republic of Iran	1,073,366
Syrian Arab Republic	1,005,472
Germany	594,269
Jordan	450,915
Kenya	402,905
Chad	347,939
China	300,986
United States	264,574
United Kingdom	238,150

REFUGEES IN THE WEST

More than 1.3 million refugees were granted citizenship in their country of asylum from 1999 to 2009. Of this number, the United States alone accounted for more than half. In 2009 the United States granted citizenship to 55,300 refugees, Belgium granted citizenship to 2,200 refugees, and Ireland, 730.[12]

Table 8.2 Primary Destination Countries of New Asylum Seekers, 2008–2009[13]

Country	New Asylum Seekers
South Africa	222,000
United States	47,900
France	42,100
Malaysia	40,000
Ecuador	35,500
Canada	34,000
United Kingdom	29,800

There were several increases in the number of asylum seekers in Europe in 2009, where claims totaled 51,100 (a 13% increase). Asylum applications increased in Denmark (59%), Finland (47%), and Norway (19%). While claims for New Zealand have remained constant over the past five years (averaging 300 per year), Australia saw an increase of 29% (6,200 claims). France experienced a 19% increase in 2009 (42,000 new applications) over 2008. This increase was partly due to the influx of asylum seekers from Serbia and Armenia. The United States registered approximately 49,000 new applications (almost the same as in 2008), making it the largest single recipient of new claims among the industrialized countries. France and the United States together received 25% of all the applications lodged in the forty-four industrialized countries studied by the United Nations. In 2009 Canada observed a 10% decrease in asylum-seeker applications yet was the third-largest recipient of applications among the industrialized nations—following the United States and France.[14]

While the United Kingdom experienced a 20% increase in net migration, the number of asylum seekers coming to Britain dropped from 25,930 (2008) to 24,485 (2009).[15] The following table shows the numbers of refugees and those seeking asylum in Western countries as of 2010.

Table 8.3 Refugees and Asylum Seekers by Western Country as of 2010[16]

Country	Refugees	Asylum Seekers (pending cases)
Australia	21,805	3,706
Austria	42,630	25,625
Belgium	17,892	18,288
Canada	165,549	51,025
Denmark	17,922	3,363
Finland	8,724	2,097
France	200,687	48,576
Germany	594,269	51,991
Hungary	5,414	367
Iceland	83	39
Ireland	9,107	5,129
Italy	56,397	4,076
Liechtenstein	92	44
Luxembourg	3,254	696
Netherlands	74,961	13,053
New Zealand	2,307	216
Norway	40,260	12,473
Portugal	384	72
Spain	3,820	2,715
Sweden	82,629	18,635
Switzerland	48,813	12,916
United Kingdom	238,150	14,880
United States	264,574	6,285

WHERE DO THEY COME FROM?

In 2009 UNHCR assistance for resettlement was provided for more than 84,000 refugees. This number was 18,000 more than the previous year and the highest number since the early 1990s. The main participants by nationality in 2009 were refugees from Myanmar (24,800), Iraq (23,000), Bhutan (17,500), Somalia (5,500), Eritrea (2,500), and the Democratic Republic of the Congo (2,500).[17] The UNHCR's report *2009 Global Trends: Refugees, Asylum-seekers, Returnees, Internally Displaced and Stateless Persons* noted that by nationality, the highest number of new claims was filed by individuals from Zimbabwe (158,200), Myanmar (48,600), Eritrea (43,400), Ethiopia (42,500), Colombia (39,200), Afghanistan (38,900), and Somalia (37,900).[18]

In forty-four industrialized countries studied by the UNHCR in 2009, Afghanistan, Iraq, Somalia, the Russian Federation, and China were the five most important source countries of asylum seekers. Afghans sought asylum in thirty-nine of the forty-four industrialized countries, with their numbers being the highest in Norway (3,900), the United Kingdom (3,500), Germany (3,300), Austria (2,200), Sweden (1,700), and Belgium (1,700). From Iraqis, Germany experienced 6,300 claims for asylum and Sweden 2,300. More than half of all asylum requests from Somalis were made to the Netherlands (5,900) and Sweden (5,900), an increase of 53% and 75% respectively as compared to 2008. Austria and France received large numbers of asylum seekers from the Russian Federation with 3,600 and 3,400 claims respectively. The United States registered over half of all Chinese asylum applications (11,600). France was the second-largest recipient, receiving 1,600 requests from Chinese.[19] The United Kingdom received 30,545 applications for asylum in 2008, mainly from those fleeing Afghanistan (14%), Zimbabwe (12%), Eritrea (9%), Iran (9%), Iraq (7%), and Sri Lanka (6%).[20]

There were 73,293 refugees who arrived in the United States in 2010. The table below reveals the nationalities and populations of the largest groups that arrived in this country.

Table 8.4 Refugee Arrivals in the US by Country of Nationality, 2010[21]

Iraq	18,016
Burma	16,693
Bhutan	12,363
Somalia	4,884
Cuba	4,818
Iran	3,543
Congo, Democratic Republic	3,174
Eritrea	2,570
Vietnam	873
Ethiopia	668
All other countries, including unknown	5,691
Total	**73,293**

DO THEY RETURN HOME?

While some refugees settle permanently in their host countries, many have plans to return home. Even among those who settle for years in another country, many have plans to return home to live indefinitely. The UNHCR estimated that in 2009 the number of refugees who voluntarily returned to their countries of origin was 251,500. Taken with the numbers of those who have returned voluntarily over the past twenty years, that leads the UNHCR to estimate that the number of returnees is 24.7 million refugees. In 2009 the main countries of return were Afghanistan (57,600), the Democratic Republic of the Congo (44,300), Iraq (38,000), Sudan (33,100), Burundi (32,400), and Rwanda (20,600). Since the large-scale return of the Afghans began in 2002, more than 5.3 million have returned home. From 2005 to 2009 there were 300,000 Sudanese refugees who returned home.[22]

CONCLUSION

As I approached the completion of this book, the North African and Middle Eastern world began experiencing unprecedented change. The peoples in countries such as Tunisia, Egypt, Bahrain, and Libya rose up to lead protests against their governments. While many were celebrating these revolutions, others were fleeing for their lives. Some of the countries experienced less violence than others; however, social dislocation was widespread. Before writing this conclusion, I decided to check the news reports of the situation in North Africa. The first story I read noted, "More than 110,000 refugees have fled Libya in the last week."[23]

Unfortunately, the peoples of the world still have to move in fear for their lives. And until the Lord returns, such will be the case. Until then, as the refugees of the world move, may the church be intentional, reaching out with compassion to those strangers who find themselves in strange lands. And may their sojourns result in true comfort, peace, and rest from the Prince of Peace.

Stories from the Field

PEOPLES ON THE MOVE

In 2007 New Zealand experienced an inflow of 2,790 people from India, 1,593 from China, and 1,409 from Japan.[1]

There are at least three million Turks living in Germany, with most of the Muslim population being Turks.[2]

It was estimated at the beginning of the twenty-first century that sixty to seventy thousand Hindus lived in Germany. In 1997 Sweden received 3,100 Gujarati Hindus.[3]

By 2004 there were 200,000 individuals from the former Yugoslavia and 155,000 people from Morocco in OECD (Organisation for Economic Co-operation and Development) countries. Africans represented about one-third of the immigrant community.[4]

■ ■ ■

For the most part, the church in the West has not caught the vision to reach the unreached peoples who have migrated to our communities, equip them, and partner with them to carry the gospel to their peoples across the world. The purpose of this chapter is to tell you about some people who have such a global vision of reaching the nations and what they have been doing. It is my hope that we will be inspired and convicted by their examples while learning from their experiences. May their stories spur us on to be greater workers for the kingdom.

HENRY SMITH: REACHING THE WORLD
FROM CALIFORNIA

Hentry Smith's (pseudonym) family immigrated to the United States from Eastern Europe when he was an infant in the 1950s. In the 1980s, Hentry and his wife were living in the San Jose, California, area when they sensed a call to serve as missionaries overseas. When they soon noticed that many refugees were living nearby, Henry's wife thought that before they left the States to serve they should immerse themselves in cross-cultural ministry in their neighborhood. After they were introduced to some Vietnamese and Cambodian families, they began teaching them English and cultural skills regarding how to integrate into American society.

During his college years, Smith had been involved in the Navigators and carried the vision of multiplication with him into his work with the refugees. "We realized that a lot of churches were sponsoring these refugees in order to incorporate them into their memberships," Smith said. "A lot of ministry was directed to these people, and they became Christians." But Smith and his wife decided to use a different approach. "We saw right away that these people were so culturally different that if they came to Christ, we believed that God wanted them to organize their own churches. So we started a church-planting ministry for these people, so their churches could have their own languages and their own cultural forms." Henry and his wife worked among many different language groups with the vision to plant churches among each group so that each group would send their people back to plant churches in their countries of origin.

One refugee who came to faith in a Thai refugee camp before settling in California was a Cambodian named Enoch (not his real name). Henry and his wife began to teach and help Enoch develop a vision for his people. Eventually, Enoch returned to Cambodia as a church planter, and at the time of this writing, Smith had visited Cambodia and noted that the planting of 803 churches could be traced to Enoch's ministry.

During our conversation, Smith observed that although many refugees come to faith after migrating to California, they are not ready to return to their home countries to plant churches. Smith said that too many of us jump to the false conclusion that they *are* ready, a notion similar to believing that all American converts immediately know how to evangelize and disciple their neighbors. Instead, the new believers need to be trained in evangelism and church planting.

Out of his work with Cambodians and also the Hmong, Smith realized the importance of partnering with those who return to their peoples. He found that in Asia, more doors would open for them if he went with them into their communities as opposed to them going alone. People would open up and talk whenever an American was present because they desired to befriend a foreigner.

For Smith, vision was critical. He noted that if a church had a vision to reach, teach, equip, partner, and send, then they were likely to see migrants return to some of the world's unreached people groups. However, if churches desired to assimilate migrants into their congregations, they rarely saw the people return with a vision and strategy for church multiplication.

When I pressed him for the names of other countries where he personally had seen such migrants to California return to plant churches, he listed Laos, Thailand, Iran, Iraq, Ethiopia, Mexico, Colombia, and India. When I inquired about the work in Iran, I was told that "hundreds, maybe thousands" of churches had been planted as a result of one man's church-planting labors in his country.

It is my desire that more and more stories like that of Henry Smith will be told. While Smith did not know what the Lord would do with the migrants who were relocated to California, there were some things that guided his thinking from the beginning. First, he had a vision for reaching, teaching, equipping, partnering, and sending the people back to their unreached peoples across the globe.

Second, this vision required that he and his wife keep their methods simple and highly reproducible among the people they reached. Third, Henry and his wife were committed to doing leadership training with the new believers. Churches planted eventually had to have qualified pastors. Fourth, they continued to partner with the people, even after seeing them return to their own countries. It was the Smiths' desire for the people and churches to be seen as their equals in ministry, not as lesser partners. At no time did I ever sense that Henry and his wife were practicing any type of paternalism over the migrants. On the contrary, they seemed to work diligently to empower and release the people for the work of the ministry.

DAVID BOYD: REACHING A GURUNG VILLAGE FROM SYDNEY'S SUBURBS

Consider the following story from David Boyd regarding the significant connection between migrants and open doors for the gospel. His work in Sydney, Australia, enabled his church to be involved in planting a church in a rural area of Nepal.

> I remember sitting in a Gurung village in the mountains of Nepal talking to a group of young men and answering their questions about the Christian faith. We were sitting in a smoke-filled room, the only light being the reflection from the fire in the center and a few candles that were scattered around. We all sat on the dirt floor, and as my friend Gam interpreted for me, I answered their questions. I marveled at what was happening as I was experiencing what most Christians would never have the chance to see. This was the very first time that the Gospel had been shared in this village! I had the privilege of bringing the Gospel message for the first time to these people.
>
> Every time someone had come to the village with a request to tell people about the "Jesus way," the elders of the village

had refused them entry. Yet as I sat there, I not only was given freedom to talk, but I had the privilege of leading the headmaster of the village school to the Lord. How did this happen? How did I, a pastor from the suburbs of Sydney, find myself in this situation? I had never considered that I had a "call" to Nepal, yet here I was visiting a member of my church in his own home and seeing firsthand what God was doing.

Gam had come to faith in Sydney and for a short time had been part of the church family. Because we took Gam into our church family, made him part of our lives and did not forget him when he returned home, the door of opportunity was there for us to walk through. This door led us to an unreached people group in a closed village; and because we were connected to a young man of influence in the village, we were able to enter as insiders, not outsiders. Even while Nepalese evangelists were refused entry, we could walk in welcomed by all the villagers.[5]

Boyd also noted that it was through Gam's witness that a church was planted in this village, with Gam as the pastor.[6]

A STORY FROM SOUTH KOREA

While the following story is not from a Western country, the vision, principles, and strategy can be appropriately contextualized to the West. In South Korea, Koreans are reaching out to the Mongolians who have migrated to their country. Myunghee Lee noted that the churches have both a vision and strategy for reaching this unreached people with the good news. According to Lee, the migrant workers' churches believe that the evangelization of the countries of origin will come about as they evangelize the migrant. The churches focus on reaching the migrants with the gospel, teaching them and training leaders, and leading them to be involved in missions. The chief director of the Diaspora Mongolian Network noted that migrant Mongolian workers are seven times more likely to become Christians than Mongolians in their home country.[7]

Another approach being used is to connect with the family members of the workers. Those ministering to the workers in Korea take trips into Mongolia once or twice each year and show pictures and videos of the workers to their families. Lee wrote: "Since Mongolians live with extended family members, over ten family members per one migrant worker gather at such occasions. In other words, about 100 people gather for ten migrant workers, and an opportunity opens up to evangelize them. When they feel relieved to see their loved ones living happily even as laborers in a foreign land and to hear that such life is the result of encountering Jesus Christ as their personal Savior, most of them accept the gospel. They are introduced to local churches or South Korean missionaries in Mongolia right away."[8]

Another means of reaching into Mongolia is by reaching the family members who visit the workers living in Korea. Visits are usually for extended periods of time, and the newly converted workers invite family members to attend worship services with them. In several cases, family members have returned to Mongolia as baptized believers in Jesus.[9]

Other leaders in the Korean church are calling for Koreans to become aware of the Great Commission opportunities found in the West. Minho Song wrote, "If the Korean churches in Spain, though only a few in number, can see the value of engaging in such a mission, the implication for the evangelization of Moroccans is significant. However, reaching the Moroccans in Morocco through returning Moroccans, as insightful and logical as it may sound, remains solely a good idea until a congregation becomes aware of the sovereign hand of God in dispersing people and acts upon it."[10]

PETE: SERVING ALBANIA AND KOSOVO
FROM NEW YORK

The social networks of migrants provide great opportunities for interaction with them and their extended relationships after they return home. Jared Looney shared about the work of Pete (pseudonym) in Albania:

Pete spent five years working as a missionary in Albania. During that time, he learned the language and the culture, but he questioned the inherently Western and especially American approaches to planting a church in Albania. He felt a relational approach congruent with Albanians' emphasis on family life was needed. After returning to the United States, he continued his work among this people group. Pete moved his family first to Staten Island where he spent his first six years in New York simply gaining trust among Albanians. With the help of church volunteers, he hosted cultural events and community meetings, and he spent time building friendships among his Albanian neighbors.

After six years of personal investment, Pete started a house church among Albanians in Staten Island. Soon after, a second Albanian-speaking church began in a home in Brooklyn. Pete eventually moved across the river to New Jersey where an additional Albanian church began meeting in a library in a church building where he also serves as a pastor.

Pete explains that the majority of Albanians don't live in Albania and that missionaries must adjust their worldview to reflect contemporary realities. Many people groups are spread across the globe, and diaspora communities may become strategic networks for many missionaries while simultaneously staying connected to national leaders in the country of origin. While working in several counties and two states across Metro New York, Pete also regularly travels to Albania and Kosovo, training leaders and helping to plant churches. His commitment to this people group has placed him in a transnational reality bridging diaspora and local contexts.[11]

SAMUEL AND YOUNG CHO: TOUCHING NEPAL FROM BALTIMORE

Do you remember the example of the Chos from the introduction? While a portion of their story was shared there, it is worth repeating with a little more detail here.[12] Samuel and Young Cho, first-generation migrants and church planters in Baltimore, Maryland, know the importance of transnational missions. Their story is also a wonderful example of the potential for an integrated approach to reaching the nations.

After meeting a Nepalese waitress and her family, the Chos planted Nepal Church of Baltimore. (In the spring of 2009, they also planted a Bhutani church in the city.) In 2008 the Chos traveled to Nepal, visiting the families of the church members in Baltimore. While there, they planted Antioch Church in Jamsa, after a family member encouraged other family members and friends to hear the good news that Samuel had to share. More than two hundred people made a profession of faith in Jesus as a result.

Within a year the Chos returned to Nepal, ministering to refugees and planting two additional churches and ordaining leadership. On this trip two hundred Nepalese, three hundred Bhutanese, and thirty-five Indians made professions of faith in Jesus. Again, on this trip transnational relationships were critical to the opening of doors for the gospel.

Samuel and Young arrived in Kathmandu and then traveled to the Morang region of Jhapa in southeast Nepal, on the outskirts of a Jhapa refugee camp. They brought with them letters and gifts from Baltimore's Nepal Church members for their relatives still living in Nepal. The Nepal families cried as they looked at the pictures of their families in Baltimore.

Apart from the relationships they had established in Baltimore, it would have been extremely difficult for the Chos to have had such wonderful opportunities to share their faith in Nepal. Such social networks are gifts from the Lord that should be used to advance the gospel.

KEITH: CONNECTING WITH SOUTHEAST ASIA VIA MANHATTAN

Jared Looney shared another story about Keith (pseudonym) and his vision to reach, equip, partner, and send:

Keith moved to Manhattan as a missionary in order to plant churches among people from countries in the least reached 10/40 window. When he first began planting a house church network in New York City, he wasn't a passionate supporter of the house church movement. Rather, he began by contemplating how to reach international students and visiting scholars studying at an Ivy League campus in Manhattan. Keith wanted to strategically reach internationals so that they could carry the gospel and continue the work of church planting when they finished their studies and returned home. He recognized that conventional church planting strategies would likely not be reproducible for new believers returning home to largely non-Christian settings. If he were to see churches multiply through the social networks of new believers, he realized that what was modeled was at least as important as what was taught. He desired to demonstrate an approach to church planting that visiting students and scholars from non-Christian societies could replicate themselves while working in the academy, government, or the corporate sector and adapt fluidly to their context in Asian cities.

At the beginning of each semester, Keith and his team meet new graduate and post-graduate students as well as visiting scholars and invite them to their homes. They begin Bible studies with those who are receptive, and in recent years they have begun to see the vision for internationally planting new house churches begin to emerge. In recent years, they have begun to adapt *Discovery Bible Study Methods* as a strategy for launching new groups on campus and overseas. New believers have returned to positions in businesses or academic institutions in major cities in China, Taiwan, and Japan. Keith regularly uses Skype to continue a mentoring and coaching relationship with converts as they share the gospel and start house churches in their home context.[13]

TED: REACHING WEST AFRICA FROM HARLEM

Ted (pseudonym) is another example of a transnational missionary who works to reach peoples in different nations. I first met Ted a few years ago, after hearing of his work in Harlem, New York. He had served as a missionary in West Africa among an unreached people group and had to return to the states due to health complications. Ted soon learned that many of those West Africans from that same people group were living in Harlem. After he and his family moved into the community, they began reaching out and serving the people there. In addition to the numerous daily opportunities that Ted has to share the gospel with those in his neighborhood, he also has an integrated strategy for reaching them in the West and in the East: "Through my relationships with the people in New York, I am able to meet their friends and family members in their country in Africa." Now Ted frequently travels to Africa but only along the social networks. This means that he stays with and travels among only the family and friends of his New York friends. He does not stay with or travel with missionaries in Africa. I'll never forget when Ted told me, "I have had more opportunities to share the gospel with West Africans in Africa by living in New York than I did in the several years that I lived in West Africa. My friends in New York vouch for me and encourage their relatives to take care of me and listen to what I have to say about God." I received the following e-mail from Ted:

I recently returned from a ten-day trip to Mali. As has become the custom, I stayed in Bamako, the capital, with the families of my friends in New York. I also visit Wassulu villages, including . . . the home of our friend Moussa. God continues to work among the Wassulu. While some people who initially professed faith in Christ have disappeared due to persecution, others are meeting weekly and maturing in their faith. In the capital, two relatives of New York friends were particularly interested in discussing the gospel at length and promised they would continue to seek God and read the Bible. Both of them, on separate occasions, told a Malian pastor friend, "Our brother in New York told us of [Ted] and said that he is a person who knows God. Our brother said that [Ted] is a Christian, but we need to get close to him and learn from him."

CONCLUSION

It is my hope that additional stories will be told in the future of churches engaging and serving such people by being involved in church planting. While there are peoples and churches that have a vision for reaching, teaching, equipping, partnering, and sending migrants across the world, such laborers are few and far between. Numerous evangelistic opportunities exist among the peoples living in the West. And with the numbers who come to faith, as well as with those kingdom citizens who migrate to the West, we will have wonderful opportunities to use our abundance to equip, train, and partner together as we serve alongside our Majority World brothers and sisters in taking the gospel to the unreached of the world.

Guidelines for Reaching the Strangers Next Door

PEOPLES ON THE MOVE

Several people groups have increased their population proportions in Australia over the past few decades. The number of overseas-born Australians was five and half million in 2010, representing 26 percent of the country's total population. In the same year, the Chinese-born (excluding Hong Kong, Macau, and Taiwan) population increased to 313,600. The Indian-born population was 239,300. The Vietnam-born population was 193,300.[1]

In 2007 New Zealand experienced an inflow of 2,790 people from India, 1,593 from China, and 1,409 from Japan.[2]

■   ■   ■

TRANSNATIONAL MISSIONS IS AN INTEGRATED APPROACH to missionary strategy. It is the recognition of the reality of international migration, the importance of social networks, and the use of travel and telecommunications to make disciples of all nations without geographical constraints. Transnational missions recognizes that reaching migrants in the host countries is critical to reaching people in their social networks across the globe. In this chapter, I wish to address some important guidelines to consider when engaging in such cross-cultural domestic missionary activities.

INTENTIONALITY

Without intentionality, rarely does anything get accomplished. A church needs to have a person to catch the vision for such missionary activity. And while the leaders of your church may not be the first to catch this vision, the Lord may very well want to use you to lead in this new area for the congregation. Without an intentional plan to reach the strangers next door, it is unlikely that they will be reached in your community.

LEARN AS YOU GO

Books are good, but there is no substitute for being in the field with the people. One important guideline to keep in mind is that you must act as a sponge, learning everything you can about the people you serve. Cross-cultural missions—yes, even in your backyard—is still about crossing cultures. Become a learner. Never believe you have "arrived" and that you know it all. Humility is not only a fundamental aspect of our walk with the Lord (Micah 6:8) but also is required in order to be a servant to others.

BE WILLING TO MAKE MISTAKES

Closely connected to these guidelines is the willingness to make mistakes. If you are not open to this, you will not reach out to others. For the reality is that we will make mistakes in the process. Of course, rare are the mistakes that are massive tragedies or the creation of heresies. Most common to us are the embarrassing acts that happen because we do not understand the people as well as we think we do. Mistakes are part of learning. We must remember that the Lord recognizes that we are not perfect; he only desires our obedience and will work through our limitations. He is able to do more through our embarrassing attempts in humility than all of our grand accomplishments done in our own strength.

BRIDGES OF GOD

Donald McGavran advocated in 1955 that the social networks among the families, tribes, and clans of the world are the bridges across which the gospel should naturally travel from person to person.[3] In the present age of migration, we must make certain that we recognize the importance of this reality. God has created people to be social beings, and international migration does not change this detail.

Many migrants of the world continue to remain in frequent contact with friends and relatives in other countries. Cell phones and the Internet allow regular, ongoing communication that was difficult and costly just a few years ago. Millions of dollars each year are sent from the West to Majority World countries. These remittances help family and friends, support businesses and communities, and improve the quality of life in other nations. It is not unusual for social networks to extend to two or more countries.

The politics of home are another significant matter in the lives of many migrants. While riding in a taxi to a New York airport, I once found myself in conversation with my Haitian driver. After hearing of his knowledge of the contemporary realities in his country of birth, I asked him if the Haitian community in New York was significantly involved in the politics of Haiti. "Oh yes," he said without hesitation. "We are very much in the know of what is happening there."

Terrence Lyons and Peter Mandaville illustrated the influence of migrants living in distant lands on the shape of the politics of home:

> In October 14, 2010, it was announced by the Transition Federal Government in Mogadishu that Mohamed Abdullahi Mohamed—a US citizen employed by New York's Department of Transportation—had been appointed prime minister of Somalia. Most candidates running for the Liberian presidency in 2005 launched their campaigns in front of audiences in the United States. That same year, in the immediate aftermath of

Ethiopia's post-election crisis, both the ruling party and the opposition sent high-level representatives to address diasporas in Europe and North America. Until its defeat last year, the diplomatic and, to some extent, military strategies of the Liberation Tigers of Tamil Elam, or LTTE, in Sri Lanka were largely determined by figures in London and Toronto.[4]

If the church works through the bridges of God, then the families, tribes, and governments of the world can be influenced by the gospel from abroad. The International Organization for Migration published the findings of a report in 2005 noting that migrants continue to maintain close contacts with those in their former homelands.[5] If these social networks remain strong among migrants, there is a greater likelihood the good news will spread among the people in the homeland.

Recognizing the importance of these bridges, Timothy Paul helps us understand the gospel dissemination potential, based on his work among South Asian Indians:

> There are approximately 120 million high caste Hindu people living in India. There will be over 3 million Hindus living in the United States and Canada by 2010. Almost all of these people are from the high castes. That means that 2.5% of the high caste population of India is relocating to North America. Furthermore, every high caste Hindu person in North America comes from a large and very connected extended family to which s/he usually remains strongly committed. In fact, a typical high caste married couple residing in the United States is connected to approximately 132 other people in their family (up to first cousin), many of whom still live in India. What this means is that the growing high caste Hindu community in North America is still strongly connected to *millions* of people in India. If North American Christ followers can enter into

authentic, sustainable faith sharing relationships with the high caste Hindu people who live around them, they have the opportunity to enter into relationship with a huge proportion of India's vast unevangelized high caste Hindu population.[6]

He continued with a specific example to illustrate his point.

Brian and Ashish (not their real names) became friends in a large northeastern city in the United States. Ashish is from a highly influential high caste family in northwest India. Brian faithfully shared Christ with Ashish, who was very open to the gospel. When Ashish's father arranged his marriage in India, Brian accompanied him to the wedding. During the two weeks that they spent in India, Brian met dozens of people from both the bride's and groom's families. Today Brian is in a living relationship with Ashish and his wife who live in the United States, and he is in touch with many of the family members who live in India. This living relationship has allowed Brian to share Christ with several people from this family.[7]

RECEPTIVITY

While the topic of a peoples' receptivity level to the gospel has been discussed for decades, few churches in the West have allowed such conversations to guide missionary strategy. The gospel is not to be withheld from anyone. But as wise stewards—unless the Spirit leads otherwise—we will want to begin working among those who are the most receptive to the good news. We should desire to begin with those peoples asking the Philippian jailer's question, "What must I do to be saved?" (Acts 16:30).

At the time of this writing, I have noticed that across the globe the Spirit has been working to heighten the receptivity of many groups to the gospel. The Nepali, many Hispanic groups, Iraqis, and Iranians are among some who, in general, seem to be more receptive than most to the good news of Jesus. Another group that is receptive at this time is the Chinese. Enoch Wan has also observed this matter and shared his observations on the Chinese:

Due to the combination of multiple factors (e.g., the demise of communism, the disappointment of PRC members with communist ideology, the decrease of government control of religion, etc.), PRC people (also the largest mission field in the world) nowadays have been very receptive to the gospel in the second half of the twentieth century. The total number of Christians in PRC was about 700,000 in 1949, when foreign missionaries were forced to leave. Since then, the growth of the Christian church in PRC has been phenomenal, though the statistical data were not consistent. The official figure released by the Religious Bureau in January 2000 was 25 million; the most conservative estimate given by chairman Han W. J. of the Three-Self Patriotic Movement in China was 13 million, and the higher estimate of *Mission Frontiers* in the June 2000 issue was 60 million.[8]

People tend to be more receptive to the gospel when they are in times of stress and transition, both situations very common among migrants. According to Sharon A. Suh, 70 percent of the Korean-American population identifies as Christian, and 40 percent of those converted to the faith *after* immigration.[9] Commenting on Taiwanese and Chinese immigrants to the United States, Jehu J. Hanciles wrote: "A goodly percentage become Christians after they arrive in the United States. High rates of conversion to Christianity are recorded also among Taiwanese and Chinese immigrants. Only 2 percent of the Taiwanese population is Christian; yet 25 to 30 percent of Taiwanese immigrants in the United States are Christian, and as many as two-thirds of the members of Taiwanese Christian congregations are converts."[10]

Based on his research in the United Kingdom, John Beya noted:

> It would be inaccurate to say that most members of the franco-
> phone African churches were practicing Christians in their
> homeland. With few exceptions, their members were con-
> verted to Christianity here in Britain. Probably half of them
> come from a Catholic background; many of them will say that
> they used to be Catholics but not truly practicing Christians.
>
> Another category had hardly anything to do with Christi-
> anity prior to coming to Britain. These people initially came to
> a diaspora church as observers but were later on drawn in by
> the welcoming atmosphere; some came to accompany friends;
> others felt home-sick and wanted to re-establish contact with
> people of their culture. They liked what they found and stayed
> on. Still others join the church as a result of miracles they have
> seen happen, either to themselves or a friend, or even an un-
> known person.[11]

While research on the matter of a peoples' receptivity to the
gospel is scarce, in 2009 the North American Mission Board and
LifeWay Research conducted an online survey of seventy-four
Christian organizations comprised of 3,757 missionaries working
among first-generation immigrants in the United States and Canada.
One of the points of investigation was this: "Among the first-generation immigrant groups with whom your organization works, please
indicate each group's overall receptivity to the gospel. Receptivity
includes both the speed and the ease with which someone who hears
the gospel responds in belief and repentance."[12] Although the
findings of this survey raise some concerns for me, I do believe the
information discovered is valuable and worth sharing. The following
table reveals the nationalities of those who were considered more
and less receptive to the gospel.

Table 10.1 Receptivity Levels by Nationality (North American Mission Board/LifeWay Research Project)

More Receptive	Less Receptive
Ecuador	Vietnam
Guatemala	Spain
Liberia	Indonesia
Honduras	India
El Salvador	Pakistan
Myanmar	Japan
Brazil	Iran
Costa Rica	Iraq
Kenya	
Mexico	

A report from the International Organization for Migration noted that as migrants integrate into the host country, "if they are not provided adequate support in their integration efforts, or if they feel isolated and in need of reaffirming their identity, migrants may move away from more modern religious values and practices observed in their country of origin towards more traditional ones in the host country." Of course the opposite is also true. Many migrants become more committed to their religions after migration. For example, the same report noted that Somali migrants to Finland became more devout, likely as a means to defend their identity.[13]

CULTURAL AND GENERATIONAL DIFFERENCES

All minorities in your country are not the same. They all arrived on your shores, but they come from a multitude of places, embracing a multitude of worldviews and lifestyles. The cultures (and subcultures) of home have helped shape them to be the people they are today. It is important that we recognize that Somalis, Mexicans, and Indians, for example, represent radically different groups. It will be very difficult—if not impossible—to relate to everyone the same way.

Not only are there cultural differences across people groups, but differences arise from generation to generation within the same group.

Second- and third-generation Koreans living in Ontario are likely to have integrated more than their parents or grandparents. They are going to be more mainstream Canadians than their elders. Speaking English and the Canadian way of doing things are more comfortable to them. These differences must be taken into consideration when working among ethnic minority groups. It is very likely that the Anglo middle-class Canadian male will have more in common with a second-generation Korean than a first-generation Korean. For the Anglo Canadians, such church-planting work will be less cross-cultural than if they were working among first-generation Koreans.

CONTEXTUALLY APPROPRIATE METHODS

It is important that the church contextualize everything it does, from evangelism to training others in church-planting methods. Donna S. Thomas shared from her experience of trying to reach some friends using a traditional American method—inviting someone to a church event:

> I made a mistake one Christmas by taking my Indian friends to my church's Christmas pageant. To me it was the wonderful story of Mary and the birth of Jesus. The music was spectacular. The costumes were beautiful. It was great for our people. But as I sat there in the sanctuary beside my Indian friends, I realized that they didn't have a clue as to what this pageant was all about. It didn't make sense to them. It confused them. Oh, how I wished I had not brought them. I sunk deeper and deeper down in the pew as the story continued. What was being sung and performed was way out of their comprehension. For non-Christians who had never heard about the birth of Jesus, it was weird, beyond their understanding. Yes, it was wonderful for all of us Christians, but not so for those who didn't already know the story.[14]

While Thomas is not opposed to inviting friends to such an event, her exhortation is important for us to heed. We must understand the people we are attempting to reach, not assuming that our preferred methods of evangelism will communicate the truth in a way they can understand. While it is important that this be kept in mind when it comes to evangelism, we should also remember that the same is true when it comes to teaching people to obey Jesus and developing leaders. We must understand the people we serve and how best to communicate with them.

In the process of reaching and teaching others, we must recognize that our cultural preferences for functioning as a church are not necessarily biblical requirements. We must be discerning, teaching these new believers what the Bible says about the local church while avoiding, as much as possible, the impartation of our cultural desires. Our approach should be to assist them in thinking through how to apply biblical principles to their contexts as they plant churches. Our goal does not involve cloning our preferences among them.

EVANGELISM THAT RESULTS IN NEW CHURCHES

Biblical church planting is evangelism that results in new churches.[15] The vision of the team that is working to reach those who have migrated to the West must have this definition in mind. While space will not permit me to enter into a discussion on church planting, I will direct you to my book *Discovering Church Planting: An Introduction to the Whats, Whys, and Hows of Global Church Planting.*

If the desired outcome is to see the peoples return to their countries of origin and make disciples across the world, they need to be reached and taught to obey the commands of Jesus in the context of church planting. It is difficult to train others in church planting if the only experience they have is in the context of a well-established church. While there are always exceptions to reaching and teaching peoples, a general principle is to do so through church-planting ministries. If this is not an option where you live, work diligently to help people understand that 1) your established church is not the only expression of the local church; 2) church planting is extremely important for global disciple making; and 3) you will provide them with some other hands-on experiences to assist in developing skills related to such missionary work.

SIMPLE STRATEGY AND
HIGHLY REPRODUCIBLE METHODS

Social organizations generally move from the simple to the complex, with churches being no exception. The Reproducibility-Potential Guide offers a visual portrait of this matter (see figure 10.1) as related to our methods for teaching people how to obey Jesus and plant churches.

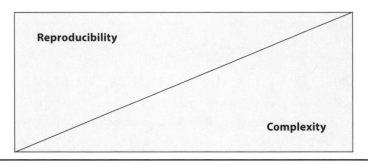

Figure 10.1 Reproducibility-Potential Guide

As our means of teaching, developing leaders, and modeling become more and more complex, the likelihood of reproduction by the migrants decreases. If they must plant churches "the American way," it will be most unlikely that they will be able to return to their peoples and plant churches with them.

This matter of keeping everything simple is going to be a *great* challenge for most churches and those working with unreached peoples in the West. Much of the way we experience church life is extremely complex, technical, and difficult to multiply. While there is nothing inherently wrong with structures and organizations and highly educated, skilled leaders, we often define a healthy local church in these culturally preferred terms that are beyond the biblical prescription.

A wealth of material aids, money, and people are not essential to plant a church. Rather, the gospel, the Holy Spirit, receptive hearts, and committed laborers among the migrants are all that are necessary (see 1 Thessalonians 1:1–10). A simple expression of the body of Christ is not necessarily unhealthy, and a complex expression of the body of Christ is not necessarily healthy. The exhortation of Charles Brock is helpful here: "From day one, the church planter should think *reproducible*. Do not provide any material crutch the people cannot provide for themselves. Is this stingy? No, it is responsible stewardship with the long-term best in mind for the people."[16]

Work to keep everything simple and radically biblical. Do not put the proverbial cart before the horse by giving the new migrant believers complex tasks and ministries. If complexity comes, let it come from them making the decisions about what is best in reaching their contexts. Allow them to grow and develop in their walk with the Lord and with others in the church.

PARTNERSHIP, NOT PATERNALISM

During the years of colonialism, Western cultural preferences were understood to be superior to those of other societies. Christianization was often equated with Westernization, which involved "civilizing" a people according to the Western way as they came to Jesus. Such paternalism naturally played out in missionary contexts. The "right way" of being and functioning as a local church was the way of the West. Worship expressions, communication styles, and organization and structures all had to come from the missionaries' cultures. The national believers in the Majority World were never seen as being capable of doing things the proper way. And it took decades before they were understood—if ever—as partners in the ministry.

While new believers should not be given free reign to follow their own desires, we must also avoid being paternalistic. It is very important that those of us in the West work alongside new believers and churches across the globe to equip them and raise them up to be cultural expressions of the body of Christ in their communities. We must make certain that we hold them to high biblical expectations but not to the expectations of our cultural preferences. Teach them the Bible. Teach them to think about their people. Teach them how to apply the gospel and church-planting methods in their own contexts.

We must work to raise up new migrant believers as partners in the gospel ministry. It is important to see them as equals, rather than as infants who are incapable of carrying the gospel and multiplying disciples, pastors, and churches across the world. We need to realize that they are more than likely able to carry the gospel farther and faster than we could among their people.

CONCLUSION

In this chapter I have provided a few guidelines to assist you and your church in getting started in reaching the strangers next door. While this chapter has just scratched the surface of the topic, my purpose throughout this book has been to provide you with an introduction to reaching the nations through migrations. It is my hope and prayer that you will keep these guidelines in mind as you begin to work in your community. Please flesh out the contents of this chapter and add more guidelines as you serve those living among you. In the next chapter I want to provide you with a simple strategy for this missionary activity.

A Suggested Strategy for Reaching the Strangers Next Door

PEOPLES ON THE MOVE

For its size, Canada has much ethnic diversity. And this diversity is only expected to increase in the future. Consider these projections for 2017:[1]

- One in five Canadians could be a visible minority person.
- Immigrant population is expected to be between 7 million and 9.3 million.
- Half of all visible minorities in Canada are expected to be Chinese or South Asian.
- The highest growth rates for visible minorities in Canada are projected for West Asians, Koreans, and Arab groups.
- 95 percent of the visible minority people are expected to live in one of Canada's metropolitan areas.
- Half of the population of Toronto and Vancouver may be visible minorities.

■ ■ ■

WITH SO MANY PEOPLES ON THE MOVE, how are local churches to respond? While there are numerous responses, I want to offer a simple, yet general, strategy I have mentioned throughout this book.[2] I refer to it as the R.E.P.S. strategy: Reach, Equip, Partner, and Send.

Whether they are working with students, people who have immigrated, or refugees, churches and mission agencies would be wise to embrace this approach for making disciples of all nations. The R.E.P.S. strategy is designed to be contextualized by churches and missionaries in their areas, among those who have migrated next door.

As I prepared to write this chapter, I read an article titled "Tunisia refugees flood Italian island" and watched a British Broadcasting Corporation video about the migration of large numbers of Chinese to Southern Africa, helping to shape the economy there.[3] In light of this chapter, I cannot help wondering what—if anything—the churches in Italy are doing to minister to the four thousand refugees who arrived in a matter of a few days and what the churches in Africa are doing as lonely Chinese construction workers live for months and years at a time in their land. Is anyone considering reaching, equipping, partnering with, and sending these men and women out with the good news of Jesus' love?

PRAYER IN ALL THINGS

Reaching the nations of the world requires that we are people of prayer. For it is out of an intimate walk with God that the church is filled with the Spirit to carry out the Great Commission (Acts 1:8). From this devotion, we receive wisdom and guidance to understand how best to relate to the strangers next door. Prayer must not be understood as something to do before putting together a strategy; rather, we are to pray without ceasing (1 Thessalonians 5:17). Without prayer, all strategies are impotent. Without prayer, strategic planning is foolishness.

REACH

Following prayer, the strategy begins by reaching people where they are in their spiritual journeys. For those who are without Jesus upon arrival, the church is to take the gospel to them. Both actions and words are to be communicated in love. Methods of connecting with migrants will vary from context to context. Some groups will teach English, driving skills, and cultural-acquisition skills and will provide other practical assistance to those with needs. Some peoples will require that we get to know them by eating, drinking, hanging out, and playing sports with them. Obviously, different peoples must be approached differently. Those who have voluntarily migrated—such as students—will have different needs than those who have been forced to migrate—such as refugees.

The church must not view migrants as a project or a way to accomplish a goal. Rather, we must understand that all peoples are created in the image of God and are to be respected—even when we disagree with one another. While we share the love of Jesus, calling all people to repent and place their faith in him, at no time are we to be coercive or manipulative. We are to care for other people whether or not they become followers of Jesus. Our service is to come with no strings attached.

Dana Chastang, director of the international student ministry at Woodland Park Baptist Church in Hammond, Louisiana, helps lead her church to reach students studying in their area. She believes the key is to work through relationships with the students. "It requires patience," she said. "You meet their needs and have patience as you minister to them." Several churches in Hammond partner to provide hospitality to the students, offering a bicycle-loan program, a food pantry, furniture donation, and even assistance with transportation. They have seen students return home to begin Bible studies.[4]

Dale Martin (pseudonym) noted that followers of Christ should establish friendship networks among Muslims migrating to Europe, with such networks assisting them in assimilating into European society. According to Martin, "If the Muslim sees the community of Christians as a viable entryway into the host culture, not only will Muslims be less likely to remain marginalized and vulnerable to Islamists, but the gospel will get a better hearing."[5]

Some questions to ask at this stage include these:

- Who do I need on my team to assist in this ministry?
- What do we know about the people (e.g., culturally, spiritually, demographically)?
- Why are they in this community?
- What are the barriers to reaching them with the gospel?
- What are the bridges to connecting with them?
- What are the best ways to share the gospel, start Bible studies, and plant churches with them?

EQUIP

The church is commanded to make disciples and teach them to obey the commands of Jesus (Matthew 28:18–20), *not* simply to make converts. It is very important that the equipping stage of the strategy involves teaching new believers both the fundamentals of the faith and leadership skills.

Whether the new believers are literate or not, they need to know how to understand and apply the Scriptures, fast and pray, share their faith, and deal with spiritual warfare. They need to understand what it means to be a part of a local church, even if that local church is initially made up of just a few other new believers. They need to understand their identity in Jesus, how to rely on the Holy Spirit, and how to rest in the assurance of their salvation in Christ. Regardless of our contexts, we must understand how to teach new believers the spiritual disciplines common to all.

Teaching obedience and leadership development go hand in hand. A good leader must be a good follower of Jesus. We need to provide opportunities for new believers to develop skills in personal evangelism, gathering and leading Bible-study groups and churches, and raising up other leaders.

While not everyone will be sent out as church planters, the equipping of these missionaries must be at the forefront of our thinking. They need to be taught how to function as the local church and to plant other churches. While the Scriptures do not provide a time line for when a new believer can plant churches or pastor churches, we do know that the apostle Paul remained in Ephesus for three years, in Corinth for eighteen months, and in other areas sometimes only a few weeks. Yet he left behind new churches comprised of new believers and their own elders. The church in the West needs to return to the Scriptures to understand that healthy churches can be planted in a much shorter time than most of us expect. We must also properly understand the grammatical and historical context of the passage that mandates a pastor "must not be a recent convert" (1 Timothy 3:6). The apostle who wrote this is the same apostle whose first missionary journey involved evangelism, church planting, and appointing elders among those churches, all within about a two-year period of time (Acts 13—14).

Part of our equipping must involve the modeling of a simple expression of the local church. As noted in the previous chapter, this will be a challenge for many of us, for our definition of a local church includes not only the biblical prescriptions but also, generally, a great deal more—many Western cultural preferences. One of the problems with such understandings of the local church is that we end up teaching new believers an unbiblical—maybe even a syncretistic—understanding of the local church. In addition to providing poor biblical teaching, we also provide complicated structures and organizations that are difficult for new believers to reproduce among their peoples across the world.

Teaching a simple model of the local church is not always an easy task. Sometimes all things Western, including the church, appeal to those from the Majority World. I once spoke with a pastor whose church had been doing an amazing job reaching Chinese students and seeing them baptized and becoming members of the church. Knowing that when the students graduated many would return to China, I asked him if he had considered the realities awaiting these new believers once they returned and attempted to find a church like his. He was well aware of the problem and had tried on several occasions to prepare the new believers for this reality. "They really enjoy the American experience," he said. "We're working on equipping them to return and plant house churches, but they enjoy the large church worship experience."

Since sometimes the novelty of Western Christian culture is attractive, we must be prepared to respond appropriately. While teaching from the Scriptures on the doctrine of the church, we need to instruct others that our culturally preferred ways are not the only ways and simultaneously help those we are teaching to think through how they will apply biblical church-planting principles to their own contexts.

Since people imitate and reproduce what they experience, those working with migrants must address this modeling challenge. While it is possible to incorporate new believers into established churches, I suggest that this be the exception rather than the norm. It would be better for churches to be planted with only a few new believers, whereby they can grow, fellowship, worship together, and form their own church-planting teams to return to other parts of the world. In this context, equipping is likely to happen at a faster rate. Accountability levels can remain high. Growth in spiritual disciplines and leadership development can happen faster than in a context where new believers may get lost in the crowd or may not understand much in a foreign context with others who have been believers for many years. Fellowship with Western believers can be accomplished through means and opportunities other than assimilating new believers into established churches.

With this in mind, the R.E.P.S. strategy includes the planting of local churches among those migrating to the West and for those churches to send out their own missionary teams to other parts of the world.

Those of us in the West can learn from David Chul Han Jun's experience and research on ministry to migrants in South Korea. He wrote:

> Therefore, if we want to make an impact through our migrant workers' mission, we have to train migrant Christian workers to become missionaries to their own people and train them to work with other missionaries already serving in their countries. We have to network with them in their native countries by supporting their church planting efforts. The domestic migrant worker mission goal has to be training them to become missionaries to their own people when they return.[6]

Some questions to ask at this stage include these:

- Now that they are believers, what is the best way to teach them the Scriptures?

- How can we hold them accountable for applying the Scriptures to their lives?

- Are we casting the vision for them to return to reach their social networks?

- How can we model spiritual disciplines and local-church involvement for them?

- After teaching them about the local church, do they believe the Spirit is leading them to unite together as a local church?

- Who might the Lord be raising up to pastor this new church?

- What are the immediate leadership skills we need to be cultivating in the lives of the leaders?

- Who might the Lord be preparing to return to their people as missionaries?

PARTNER

Just as Jesus never abandoned his church and sent the Holy Spirit, and just as the apostle Paul wrote letters to new churches, returned to visit them, and sent others to visit them—the third stage of the strategy involves developing healthy partnerships with the new churches and with those who will return to their people.

It is important that the church in the West recognizes that a healthy relationship requires a true partnership. While those from Majority World contexts will know their contexts better than those living in the West, the church in the West will, no doubt, have some wisdom, exhortation, and teaching to contribute.

Also, partnership does not mean theological or missiological compromise. It is very easy to get so caught up in wanting to work with Majority World believers without being paternalistic that we embrace a laissez-faire approach to partnership. Unfortunately, there are some misguided individuals who advocate that everything coming from Majority World churches is healthy and that the West should not have any say in the matter of world evangelization.

While I do not agree that everything that comes from the West is good, I also do not agree that everything in the West is bad; and I definitely do not believe that everything found among Majority World churches is healthy. The Lord has not given up on the church in the West. He also has blessed us with a great wealth of resources (e.g., people, money, experience, wisdom, education, institutions) for encouraging and edifying our brothers and sisters. Healthy partnerships avoid theological and missiological compromises, treat each party as equals in the kingdom, and require accountability for all parties involved.

The extent and details of partnerships will differ from people to people, so there is a great need for prayer and healthy conversations regarding expectations. Those in the West should not be paternalistic, and they also should not enter into partnerships that would cause the migrants to become dependent on them—even if it is what the Majority World believers desire.

Some questions to ask at this stage include these:

- Are we treating the new church as partners in the gospel ministry?

- What do all parties believe are the necessary components for healthy partnership?

- What should they expect from us, and what should we expect from them?

- How will we continue the encouraging, training, and coaching after they return to their people?

- Does the partnership avoid both paternalism and a hands-off approach from us?

- Does the partnership encourage the growth and development of the new believers and their church?

SEND

Whether migrants come to faith in Jesus after they arrive in the West or they arrive as followers of our Lord, we must work with them to reach the nations with the gospel. Like many churches in the West, many believing migrants arrive with no vision to reach others with the gospel. Someone needs to challenge them to consider the lostness of their people and the need to return and reach the unreached nations.

I have heard from others who have worked with migrants that after they arrive in the West, they do not wish to leave. For example, Gerrie ter Haar commented on her observations in Europe:

> African Christians in Europe, as far as I have been able to detect, do not look back to the African past while spiritually and physically preparing for their return to the continent of their birth. On the contrary, they are generally forward-

looking people who use all their physical and spiritual resources to secure a better future in Europe for themselves and
their families. They have lived in Africa and they know its
condition. . . . In other words, at the present time, their
promised land is not Africa, but Europe, and the belief in a
return of African migrants to Africa appears to exist chiefly in
the minds of non-Africans, notably European policy-makers.[7]

The blessings and opportunities found in the West rightly appeal to
migrants. While I do not disagree with ter Haar's comments, we must
not underestimate God's calling on a person's life. The God who calls
the middle-class Anglo-American to leave his or her comfortable way
of life and move to a hut in the Amazonian jungle is the same Lord
over the migrant to the West. The Lord can and still calls and moves
people from lands of wealth back to Majority World countries.

Ongoing partnership with those who return to the unreached
peoples of the world is essential. Believers and churches in the West
need to continue the relationships, including traveling to work for
extended periods with the migrants who returned. I recently spoke
with one individual who shared that because the nationals desired to
show hospitality to him (the foreigner), more witnessing opportunities opened for the returning migrant when he had his American
friend present.

Some questions to ask at this stage include these:

- How do we assist migrants to return to their peoples across the globe?

- How do we travel with them to assist them in the planting of
  churches in other parts of the world?

- Are we sending long-term missionaries to serve alongside them in
  church-planting endeavors?

- What are our plans for remaining in contact with them for ongoing encouragement, training, and coaching?

CONCLUSION

A strategy for reaching the nations through international migrations does not have to be a complex matter—the more simple the strategy, the better. The R.E.P.S. strategy to engage migrants with the gospel, plant churches, and partner with them as they take the gospel across the globe is one simple approach to such labors. While the details of each stage in the strategy will vary from church to church and personality to personality, the components of reaching, equipping, partnering, and sending should be evident.

Diaspora Missiology

A Conclusion or Just the Beginning?

■ ■ ■

Not far from the central area of the German city of Hannover is a Baptist church that houses a Spanish-speaking congregation under the pastoral care of José Antonio González. Like many young people from Spain in the 1960s, José Antonio left his beautiful town in Galicia and emigrated to Germany in search of a job. There he was befriended by Mrs. Pinto, a Bolivian lady whose family had also gone to Germany in search of economic security. She not only provided José Antonio with good spiced soups but also insisted on sharing the gospel of Jesus Christ and praying for him. As a nominal Catholic, José Antonio had never thought that this story—part of the folksong heritage of his native Spain—could have any relevance for an aspiring student of industrial design. But eventually, the story of Jesus started to make sense to José Antonio, and he became a Christian believer. What he could not have dreamed was that he would eventually discern a call to the ministry and, after seminary training, become a pastor and preacher. I do not know how the gospel crossed seas to reach Mrs. Pinto in distant Bolivia, the heart of South America, but I am thrilled by the fact that when this simple Bolivian migrant housewife crossed the sea to go to Germany, she became a missionary.[1]

Samuel Escobar's account of such activity in Germany is related to a burgeoning area in the field of missions known as *diaspora missiology*. Issues such as globalization, urbanization, and the large migrations of peoples have led missiologists to begin looking at the church and the Great Commission from a different angle, asking how global issues relate to the rapid dissemination of the gospel and the multiplication of churches. Diaspora missiology is an integrated discipline, bringing migration research to bear on the study of missions. While I have not used these words to describe *Strangers Next Door*, the truth is this book is about diaspora missiology.

At the time of this writing, there are a growing number of international missiologists, missionaries, and church leaders addressing this topic. In October 2010 over four thousand evangelical leaders gathered in Cape Town, South Africa, as part of the Third Lausanne Congress on World Evangelization. One of the numerous topics addressed was migrations and mission. Under the leadership of Sadiri Joy Tira, Lausanne senior associate for diasporas, a global network of diaspora specialists produced an excellent booklet addressing biblical, theological, missiological, and practical issues related to diaspora missions. The resource, *Scattered to Gather: Embracing the Global Trend of Diaspora*, was released at the event in Cape Town and is an excellent place to begin understanding this growing field.[2]

Diaspora missiology is a complement to, not a substitute for, the traditional approach of sending missionaries to other lands. It is an approach to thinking about the missionary work of the church from an integrated perspective—including the sending of cross-cultural missionaries to work with the migrants who return.

One of the leading pioneers in this area is Enoch Wan, who has written extensively on this topic. According to Wan, "the traditional missiological distinction between 'foreign missions' and local missions is to be replaced by a 'multi-directional' approach to Christian missions."[3] Gone are the days when we should think only about sending missionaries *over there;* we must now consider how we can both get to the unreached peoples *over there* while simultaneously working to reach them *over here.* And with the migration of many followers of Jesus to the West, diaspora missiology involves training and partnering with those brothers and sisters as they work to carry out the Great Commission. This integrated approach to understanding international and domestic missionary strategy is a matter of good stewardship and is important for gospel expansion.

In an attempt to explain the strategic importance of diaspora missions, the Lausanne Diaspora Leadership Team challenged the church to consider missions to, through, and beyond the diasporas.[4]

MISSIONS TO THE DIASPORAS

Many of the world's unreached peoples have migrated not only to the West but also to many countries of the Majority World, offering the church there wonderful Great Commission opportunities to respond in love, service, and sharing the faith. Many of the strangers next door are the keys to unlocking doors into the lostness of people you and I never will be able to meet. Since I have written much throughout this book on the notion of missions to the diasporas, I will move on to the next area of consideration.

MISSIONS THROUGH THE DIASPORAS

Often, migrants desire to return home. In the late twentieth and early twenty-first centuries, many refugees, displaced persons, and other migrants returned to their countries of origin. Ellen Oxfeld and Lynellyn D. Long wrote that of the thirty million people admitted to the United States between 1900 and 1980, ten million (one-third) returned home. Referencing the United Nations High Commission for Refugees, they noted that from the 1990s to 2004 there was a steady rise in the number of refugee returns as well.[5]

Such is not the case only for refugees. Writing on Brazilians in the

United States, Maxine L. Margolis commented that the vast majority living in New York understand themselves to be "sojourners" and not "permanent residents." She continued: "Most plan to stay in New York for anywhere from two to ten years and then return to Brazil. . . . Even those few Brazilians who have lived in New York for years invariably plan to retire to their homeland."[6]

Missions through the diasporas refers to the diasporic believers returning to their countries to share the good news and plant churches among their peoples. According to the Lausanne Diaspora Leadership Team, "Christians living in the diaspora context represent the largest self-supporting contingency of missionary force which has been located within many of the so-called 'unreached peoples' and accessible to practically all people-groups of the world today."[7]

Again, since the majority of this book addresses the topic of sending the diasporas back to their peoples, I will spend the rest of this chapter on the third area of consideration.

MISSIONS BEYOND THE DIASPORAS

The concept of missions beyond the diasporas refers to the notion that diasporic believers are not only called to reach their own peoples but also are to be involved in cross-cultural missionary labors. Many Americans are not aware of the fact that there are a large number of followers of Jesus who are migrating to the West from Majority World countries, with some understanding themselves to be on mission in their new homelands. Claudia Währisch-Oblau noted that this lack of awareness is also present in Germany, with churches not recognizing that "more and more immigrants in Germany see themselves as missionaries who are to evangelize Germans."[8]

We in the West must not fool ourselves into believing that we are the only missionaries in the world today. Jason Mandryk noted, "Nearly every country is a missionary-sending country. What used to happen 'from the West to the rest' is now an extensive and expanding global activity. Missionary vision is alive even in those countries where the church is young, small or under persecution."[9] Table 12.1 reveals some of the countries that currently have out more than five hundred missionaries.

Table 12.1 Select Countries Sending More Than Five Hundred Missionaries[10]

Country	Missionaries
United States	93,500
India	82,950
China, PRC	20,000
South Korea	19,950
Nigeria	6,644
United Kingdom	6,405
Canada	5,200
Philippines	4,500
Australia	3,193
Germany	3,144
Indonesia	3,000
Ghana	2,000
Netherlands	2,000
Brazil	1,976
Switzerland	1,712
Ukraine	1,599
New Zealand	1,200
Finland	908
Sweden	873
Mexico	794
Singapore	693
Norway	610
Spain	512
Bangladesh	500

Do not be surprised when you meet a missionary sent to your Western country to do evangelism and plant churches. I remember when I first met such a person. I was in Louisville, Kentucky, and the person was a young Chinese student. He had come to the United States as a missionary from China, and his focus was not to reach the Chinese living in the city but to reach United States citizens.

Jehu J. Hanciles recognized that the large migrations of believers from their countries of birth provide a great opportunity for gospel advancement. He went as far as stating that "*the most significant counterforce to Islam in Europe is likely to come less from secularism or from Europe's homegrown, fairly moribund Christianity than from the steady influx of Christian immigrants (from Africa, Latin America, and Asia).*"[11] Jan A. B. Jongeneel noted that while the number of Muslim migrants outnumbers those migrants who claim to be Christians, he estimates there may be at least one million migrants in Europe who come from Eastern Orthodox, Roman Catholic, and Protestant traditions.[12] If there is such a large number of kingdom citizens on the move toward the West, then the church in the West must be prepared to partner with them to take the gospel to the nations.

One diasporic group heavily engaged in cross-cultural missionary activity in virtually any context into which they migrate is the Filipinos. Presently, Filipino evangelicals are scattered across the globe, laboring in the Western, Buddhist, Islamic, and Jewish worlds. Consider the following example from Canada:

My wife Linda and I lived in downtown Toronto in a condominium for three years. One of Linda's first concerns was to find a hairdresser with whom she felt comfortable, whose shop was within walking distance, and whose price was right! She started going to a hair salon run by a Filipino lady. As they started talking, Linda discovered that this vivacious woman was a genuine Christian. A few months later, Linda ended up getting her hair done by a Chinese lady at the shop. Never failing to take advantage of a God-given witnessing opportunity, Linda mentioned that her husband was pastoring the English-speaking congregation of a Chinese church in the city. The woman exclaimed, "That's great! I'm a Christian too. My boss led me to faith in Christ."

In subsequent months, Linda returned to having her hair done by the manager of the salon, the Filipino woman. But one day, a new hairdresser was at work, and since all the other operators were busy, Linda ended up with the new lady. Linda knew enough about features to discern that this beautiful woman was Somali. She asked, "Are you Somali?" Surprised, the woman blurted out, "Yes!" Knowing that Somalians are, for the most part, Muslim, Linda was well into a friendly conversation that would lead to an opportunity to share her faith. But the Somali lady declared, "Don't worry. I believe in Jesus too. That lady introduced me to the Saviour," pointing to her Chinese colleague.[13]

Many within the African diaspora are embracing their Great Commission opportunities as they migrate. For example, Hanciles wrote that the concept of America being a mission field is a real and present reality among African immigrant pastors and their congregations.[14] However, this African perspective is not limited only to the United States. Gerrie ter Haar noted that "African church leaders in Europe are today convinced of their mission to bring the gospel back to those who originally provided them with it. For many African Christians, therefore, migration to Europe is not just an economic necessity, but also seen as a God-given opportunity to evangelize among those whom they believe to have gone astray."[15]

Those of us in the West must use our blessings to equip and partner with such migrants to take the gospel to the nations. A failure to labor together is a detriment to the mission of the church. The Lord has allowed the gospel to penetrate large numbers in the Majority World so that they may now assist us in reaching the post-Christianized countries in which we live.

In addition, we must recognize another reality also. Due to the history of the Crusades and to much of the secular and ungodly cultural expression of Western society well-known throughout the

Islamic world, the predominately Anglo (white) churches of the West are likely to continue to experience many challenges to reaching the Muslim context. However, much anecdotal evidence seems to support that many Hispanic, Asian, and African peoples are over-coming these barriers because they lack the cultural history in which many such problems exist. Their physical appearances and languages do not mark them as Westerners in the traditional sense, oftentimes opening doors that their Anglo brothers and sisters of the West cannot.

Winston Smith referred to these migrants as "*bridge peoples,* bi-cultural people who, because of their dual ethnic identities, fit in both their home countries and their new locations." Smith noted that we need to enter into partnerships with these peoples in order to reach the unreached. They possess "unique cultural connections," he has said, to peoples with whom we may be unable to connect. He wrote:

For example, as a result of the Moors controlling Spain for over seven hundred years, there are more than four thousand words in Spanish that originate from the Arabic language. In fact, most of what we think of as Hispanic culture, food, language, architecture, and dance is influenced by Arabic and Jewish cultures. Is it an accident that God is bringing millions of Latinos to the United States "for such a time as this"? Could they be some of the ones God will use to finally bring the gospel to the peoples of the 10/40 Window?[16]

We in the West must recognize that the kingdom citizens migrating to our communities may be the means to sharing the love of Jesus with some of the peoples who have been the most challenging to us.

CONCLUSION

This book has been about casting a vision concerning the nations of the world. I hope the importance of being involved in missions to, through, and beyond the diasporas is now part of your thoughts about missions. Yet my desire is not for you simply to continue to *think* about these matters, but rather for you to engage the peoples of this world with the hope of Jesus. For many of us today, the opportunity to reach the nations of this world begins with us simply looking around our communities.

Global migrations provide a Great Commission opportunity for us and our churches. The international movement of the peoples of this age is part of a divine process that will result in the peoples of this world gathering around the throne. Though the Scriptures begin with a handful of people living in the home of Adam and Eve, it ends with heaven being populated with multitudes of ethnic and language groups (Revelation 5:9; 7:9). So, just as we began this book, we will also conclude it knowing that

> the God who made the world and everything in it, being Lord of heaven and earth, does not live in temples made by man, nor is he served by human hands, as though he needed anything, since he himself gives to all mankind life and breath and everything. And he made from one man every nation of mankind to live on all the face of the earth, having determined allotted periods and the boundaries of their dwelling place, that they should seek God, and perhaps feel their way toward him and find him. Yet he is actually not far from each one of us. (Acts 17:24–27)

In light of our age of migration, may the words of Paul coupled with the grand story of God's redemption move us so that the strangers next door may become our brothers and sisters in Christ, as we partner together to see the nations adopted into the family of God (Ephesians 1:5).

Appendix 1

Unreached People Groups in the United States and Canada (Global Research)

Country	People Group	Population
Canada	Quebecois	7,010,030
Canada	Walloon	32,101
Canada	Fleming	2,309
Canada	Frisian	4,400
Canada	Pennsylvania Dutch	16,902
Canada	Greek	124,500
Canada	Hungarian	77,847
Canada	Italian	483,034
Canada	Maltese	6,799
Canada	Moldovan	5,844
Canada	Romanian	89,046
Canada	English Gypsy	3,210
Canada	Danish	35,848
Canada	Icelander	2,197
Canada	Swede	8,726
Canada	Belarussian	685
Canada	Russian	141,793
Canada	Ukrainian	141,361
Canada	Bosnian	13,577
Canada	Bulgar	28,937
Canada	Croat	58,734
Canada	Macedonian	19,770
Canada	Serb, Orthodox	54,849
Canada	Serb, Muslim	13,274
Canada	Slovene	13,943
Canada	Czech	25,954
Canada	Pole	224,167
Canada	Slovak	19,978
Canada	Spaniard	11,034
Canada	Djiboutian	557
Canada	Oromo	2,542
Canada	Tigrigna	7,547
Canada	Somali	29,006
Canada	Jew, German	17,297
Canada	Jew, Israeli	18,720
Canada	Grenadian	9,846
Canada	Dutch Caribbean	2,043
Canada	Paraguayan	8,152
Canada	Belizean	2,277
Canada	Bolivian	4,299
Canada	Chilean	28,721

Country	People Group	Population
Canada	Costa Rican	3,928
Canada	Cuban	9,973
Canada	Guatemalan Mestizo	18,177
Canada	Honduran	5,695
Canada	Mexican	65,640
Canada	Nicaraguan Mestizo	9,814
Canada	Peruvian	24,671
Canada	Puerto Rican	435
Canada	Uruguayan Spaniard	7,590
Canada	Venezuelan	12,085
Canada	El Salvadoran Mestizo	44,653
Canada	Panamanian Mestizo	3,100
Canada	Brunei	4,761
Canada	Pampango	2,176
Canada	Malagasy	2,357
Canada	Malay	10,079
Canada	Barbadian	16,098
Canada	Saint Vincentian	10,721
Canada	Trinidadian	66,669
Canada	West Indian Black	7,526
Canada	Central Arctic Eskimo	3,056
Canada	Eskimo, Alaskan, Northwest	10,194
Canada	Inuinnaqtuan	387
Canada	Inukitut	53,591
Canada	Abenaki	2,247
Canada	Algonquin	6,205
Canada	Atikamek	5,573
Canada	Chinook Wawa	151
Canada	Haisla	1,285
Canada	Heiltsuk	1,660
Canada	Huron	1,605
Canada	Kitimat	225
Canada	Kutchin	2,930
Canada	Kutenai	321
Canada	Kwakiutl	338
Canada	Lakota	12,840
Canada	Malecite	1,801
Canada	Nisga'a	722
Canada	Nootka, West Coast People	4,844
Canada	Northwestern Ojibwa	22,537
Canada	Papago-Pima	676
Canada	Potawatomi	5,136
Canada	Seneca	6,421
Canada	Slave, Tinne	6,607
Canada	Southern Carrier	563
Canada	Squamish	2,592

Country	People Group	Population
Canada	Upper Tanana	282
Canada	Western Cree	59,722
Canada	Oceania	955
Canada	Tongan	1,582
Canada	Kurd, Northern	8,131
Canada	Pashto	12,738
Canada	Persian	142,329
Canada	Tajik	626
Canada	Bengali	48,496
Canada	Gujarati	86,477
Canada	Hindi	83,048
Canada	Sikh	386,251
Canada	Kannada	2,744
Canada	Konkani	3,004
Canada	Malayali	12,659
Canada	Marathi	5,101
Canada	Nepalese	3,869
Canada	Sindhi	10,992
Canada	Sinhalese	10,812
Canada	Telugu	6,968
Canada	Urdu	154,775
Canada	Lao	14,798
Canada	Khmer	20,275
Canada	Thai	5,929
Canada	Vietnamese	150,343
Canada	Bissau-Guineans	80
Canada	Wolof	1,146
Canada	Lingala	3,248
Canada	Rundi	3,434
Canada	Rwandan	3,280
Canada	Zambian	2,951
Canada	Mozambican	1,157
Canada	Ugandan	12,059
Canada	Shona	1,990
Canada	Zimbabwean	6,544
Canada	Comoros	58
Canada	Swahili	8,423
Canada	Akan	701
Canada	Beninese	913
Canada	Edo	1,189
Canada	Guinean	2,484
Canada	Ivoirians	3,116
Canada	Nigerian	15,610
Canada	Igbo	2,192
Canada	Malian	1,040
Canada	Cape Verdean	228

Country	People Group	Population
Canada	Mauritian	10,546
Canada	Reunionese Creole	138
Canada	Seychellese Creole	955
Canada	Burkina Faso	701
Canada	Gambian	499
Canada	Kenyan	16,432
Canada	Liberian	1,550
Canada	Malawian	531
Canada	Nigerien	334
Canada	Sierra Leonean	3,131
Canada	Tanzanian	21,352
Canada	Bhutanese	138
Canada	Burmese	5,297
Canada	Tibetan	4,538
Canada	Azerbaijani	1,911
Canada	Kazakh	7,027
Canada	Kyrgyz	1,369
Canada	Turk	25,981
Canada	Turkmen	244
Canada	Uzbek	2,903
United States	Arab, Persian Gulf	19,105
United States	Arab, Saudi	10,182
United States	Mauritanian	2,513
United States	Arab, Iraqi	569,921
United States	Arab, Jordanian	52,729
United States	Arab, Lebanese	519,786
United States	Arab, Palestinian	76,115
United States	Lebanese Druze	1,051
United States	Libyan	6,040
United States	Arab, Algerian	12,265
United States	Arab, Moroccan	80,278
United States	Arab, Tunisian	7,133
United States	Arab, Sudanese	37,774
United States	Arab, Yemeni	5,383
United States	Assyrian	75,694
United States	Senaya	451
United States	Arabic, Najdi Spoken	13,577
United States	Arab, Egyptian	269,129
United States	Hakka	1,155
United States	Okinawan	13,522
United States	Mongolian	8,599
United States	Oirat, Western Mongol	1,619
United States	Gheg	12,643
United States	Tosk	95,705
United States	Irish, Gaelic	31,138
United States	Scottish, Gaelic	1,931

Country	People Group	Population
United States	Welsh	3,196
United States	Armenian	246,423
United States	Latvian, Lett	23,885
United States	Lithuanian	44,024
United States	Basque	3,346
United States	Adyghe	5,345
United States	Georgian	11,865
United States	Karachay	812
United States	Estonian	6,303
United States	Finnish, Finn	27,394
United States	Breton	54
United States	French	1,771,882
United States	French-Canadian	123,148
United States	Austrian	71,722
United States	Flemish	17,848
United States	Leichtensteiner	68
United States	Low German, Plautdietsch	13,493
United States	Luxemburgher	2,423
United States	Western Frisian	976
United States	Greek	430,524
United States	Greek Cypriot	9,315
United States	Hungarian	141,996
United States	Italian	1,213,680
United States	Romansch	121
United States	Maltese	9,646
United States	Moldovian	21,984
United States	Romani, Vlax	3,093
United States	Danish	31,557
United States	Icelander	6,813
United States	Norwegian	66,758
United States	Swede	81,430
United States	Belarussian	74,219
United States	Russian	736,225
United States	Ukrainian	155,482
United States	Bosnian	111,292
United States	Bulgar	59,331
United States	Croat	70,279
United States	Macedonian	23,067
United States	Serb	54,614
United States	Slovene	11,747
United States	Czech	84,854
United States	Lusatian	301
United States	Pole	803,303
United States	Slovak	49,709
United States	Spaniard	74,192
United States	Djiboutian	276

Country	People Group	Population
United States	Amhara, Ethiopian	152,279
United States	Eritrean	19,736
United States	Somali	40,295
United States	Black Jew	47,975
United States	Jew, Bukharic	62,436
United States	Jew, Israeli	235,155
United States	Jew, Russian	104,060
United States	Jew, Spanish	130
United States	Jew, Syrian	52,030
United States	Jew, Tehrani	10,406
United States	Yiddish	215,379
United States	Afro-Seminole	200
United States	Patois	29,631
United States	Surinamer	6,288
United States	French Guiana	327
United States	Bari, Motilon	958
United States	Carib, Galibi	4,507
United States	Curipaco	237
United States	Aztec	6,752
United States	Cora	520
United States	Yaqui	746
United States	Costa Rican	80,985
United States	Uruguayan Spaniard	28,210
United States	Eastern Kanjobal, Conob	74,961
United States	Mayan	9,171
United States	Mixteco, Alcozauca	21
United States	Cocopa	690
United States	Kumiai	119
United States	Misumalpan	180
United States	Tarascan	1,029
United States	Quechua	1,065
United States	Arawak	4,028
United States	Carib Motilon, Yukpa	634
United States	Piapoco	112
United States	Puinave	270
United States	Zapoteco	32
United States	Achenese	140
United States	Balinese	151
United States	Brunei	699
United States	Pampangan	6,674
United States	Pangasinan	2,450
United States	Bicolano	535
United States	Javanese	216
United States	Malagasy	288
United States	Indonesian	5,967
United States	Malay	12,842

Country	People Group	Population
United States	Bahamian	31,641
United States	Barbadian	58,789
United States	Montserrat	4,400
United States	Eskimo Creole	2,998
United States	Eskimo, Alaska Inupiat, Northwest	4,507
United States	Eskimo, Alaskan, North	10,794
United States	Eskimo, St Lawrence Island, Siorarmiut	1,349
United States	West Alaskan Eskimo, Central Yupik	23,178
United States	Achumawi, Pitt River	1,000
United States	Ahtena, Copper River	500
United States	Alabama	518
United States	Algonquian	620
United States	Apache, Jicarilla	2,699
United States	Apache, Kiowa	1,349
United States	Apache, Lipan	113
United States	Apache, Mescalero	2,699
United States	Apache, Western	16,281
United States	Arapaho	6,777
United States	Arikara	94
United States	Atsugewi	200
United States	Caddo	51
United States	Cahuilla	1,079
United States	Catawba	500
United States	Cayuga	1,199
United States	Chehalis	200
United States	Cherokee	316,716
United States	Cheyenne	5,997
United States	Chikasaw	40,566
United States	Chinook Wawa	150
United States	Chitimacha	300
United States	Choctaw	98,427
United States	Chumash	113
United States	Columbia River Sahaptin	150
United States	Columbia-Wenatchi	690
United States	Comanche	8,185
United States	Creek, Muskogee	27,256
United States	Crow	8,636
United States	Dakota, Sioux	23,988
United States	Degexit'an, Ingalik	420
United States	Eastern Keres Pueblo	6,806
United States	Eastern Ojibwa, Chippewa	5,707
United States	Flathead-Kalispel	4,078
United States	Haida	1,349
United States	Hidatsa	1,499
United States	Hopi, Hopitu-Shinumu	8,846
United States	Houma, Half-Choctaw	4,378

Country	People Group	Population
United States	Iowa	2,704
United States	Jemez	2,728
United States	Kansa	83
United States	Karok	4,858
United States	Kashaya	56
United States	Kickapoo	2,038
United States	Kiowa	8,185
United States	Kitsai	394
United States	Koasati	1,349
United States	Koyukon	2,998
United States	Kutchin, Gwichin	607
United States	Kutenai	208
United States	Lakota	11,994
United States	Luiseno	2,254
United States	Lumbee	40,898
United States	Lushootseed	2,254
United States	Makah	809
United States	Maricopa	451
United States	Massachusett, Wampanoag	4,246
United States	Menomini	4,768
United States	Miami	2,728
United States	Mikasuki Seminole	1,650
United States	Mitchif, French Cree	259
United States	Miwok	420
United States	Mohave	2,038
United States	Mohegan-Montauk-Narragansett	1,919
United States	Nanticoke	540
United States	Navaho	303,344
United States	Nez Perce	2,038
United States	Nooksack	480
United States	Northeast Sahaptin	700
United States	Northern Tiwa, Picuris	2,728
United States	Omaha-Ponca, Dhegiha	6,781
United States	Onondaga	899
United States	Otoe, Chiwere	1,739
United States	Oto-Manguen	6,939
United States	Pacific Yupik, Aleut	4,078
United States	Paiute, Northern	4,917
United States	Paiute, Southern	6,806
United States	Panamint	100
United States	Passamaquoddy, Malecite	1,800
United States	Penobscot	1,199
United States	Pomo	5,359
United States	Potawatomi	4,497
United States	Powhatan	4,078
United States	Quapaw	159

Country	People Group	Population
United States	Quechan, Kechan	2,038
United States	Salish, Southern Puget	1,482
United States	Sauk-Fox, Mesquakie	3,418
United States	Seneca	5,997
United States	Shawnee	2,728
United States	Shoshoni	9,535
United States	Skagit	480
United States	Southern Tiwa	4,078
United States	Spokane	1,349
United States	Tanacross	120
United States	Tanaina	798
United States	Tanana	380
United States	Tenino, Warm Springs	1,000
United States	Tewa	4,611
United States	Tonkawa	119
United States	Tunica	210
United States	Twana	480
United States	Upland Yuman	2,038
United States	Upper Chinook	750
United States	Upper Kuskokwim, Ingalik	210
United States	Upper Piman, Papago-Pima	27,256
United States	Upper Tanana, Tanacross	630
United States	Western Cree	29,985
United States	Western Keres Pueblo	10,914
United States	Winnebago	6,761
United States	Wiyot	507
United States	Yakima	10,914
United States	Yokuts, Chuckchansi	2,500
United States	Zuni Pueblo	10,874
United States	Chamorro	19,091
United States	Gilbertese	187
United States	Kusaiean	686
United States	Micronesian	5,853
United States	Midway Islanders	2,542
United States	Mokilese	466
United States	Palau	2,810
United States	Ponapean	1,625
United States	Trukese	2,726
United States	Yapese	704
United States	Melanesian	1,152
United States	French Polynesian	1,228
United States	Hawai'I Creole-speakers	180
United States	Maori	313
United States	Marquesan	349
United States	Niuean	66
United States	Polynesian	13,675

Country	People Group	Population
United States	Rarotongan	78
United States	Tokelauan	85
United States	Balochi	279
United States	Kurd, Central	12,264
United States	Pashto	17,509
United States	Afghan	70,031
United States	Iranian	302,807
United States	Mashadis	4,683
United States	Tadzhik	156
United States	Assamese	1,264
United States	Bengali	197,808
United States	Bihari	151
United States	Gujarati	284,039
United States	Hindi	381,609
United States	Kannada	29,356
United States	Kashmiri	1,137
United States	Malayali	96,114
United States	Marathi	42,139
United States	Munda	2,429
United States	Nepalese	12,891
United States	Oriya	2,846
United States	Punjabi	170,599
United States	Rajasthani	403
United States	Sindhi	9,407
United States	Sinhalese	16,718
United States	Tamil	101,060
United States	Telugu	103,708
United States	Muhajir	273,564
United States	Urdu	257,270
United States	Tjam	1,108
United States	Lao	450,000
United States	Boloven	36,058
United States	Brao	101
United States	Khmer, Cambodian	218,924
United States	Khuen	3,042
United States	Lamet	27
United States	Tai Lu	4,507
United States	White Tai	11,994
United States	Black Tai	4,507
United States	Thai	191,335
United States	Vietnamese	1,215,190
United States	Iu Mien	27,044
United States	Yao	25,917
United States	Tho	599
United States	Central Africans	259
United States	Wolof	62,436

Country	People Group	Population
United States	Equatorial Guineans	338
United States	Gabonese	462
United States	Burundi	9,365
United States	Luba-Kasai (Zaire)	5,623
United States	Zambian	6,750
United States	Mozambican	2,282
United States	Ugandan	13,229
United States	Swazi	535
United States	Zimbabwean	12,040
United States	Basotho	276
United States	Efik	6,349
United States	Chadic	3,875
United States	Fulani	15,105
United States	Fulbe Futa	7,805
United States	Futa Toro	2,602
United States	Ghanaian	73,888
United States	Togolese	3,149
United States	Khoisan	78
United States	Mandinka	2,602
United States	Maninka	5,203
United States	Bambara	5,203
United States	Malian	3,082
United States	Jula	5,203
United States	Mande	14,853
United States	Anuak	2,576
United States	Dinka	7,160
United States	Jur	1,885
United States	Nilotic	4,183
United States	Nuer	16,079
United States	Shilluk	5,656
United States	Uduk	349
United States	Botswanan	1,555
United States	Liberian	43,980
United States	South African	52,351
United States	Soninke	5,203
United States	Ivorian	2,451
United States	Malawian	1,724
United States	Namibian	947
United States	Nubian	4,008
United States	Rwandan	2,734
United States	Azande	12,052
United States	Kaliko	180
United States	Moru	2,576
United States	Bhutanese	366
United States	Burmese	23,711
United States	Karen	288

Country	People Group	Population
United States	Kachin	78
United States	Tibetan	10,160
United States	Azerbaijani	6,257
United States	Kazakh	240
United States	Kyrgyz	60
United States	Meskhetian Turk	9,554
United States	Turk	85,484
United States	Turkish Cypriot	3,175
United States	Turkmen	205
United States	Eastern Aleut	2,699
United States	Tatar	7,000
United States	Uyghur	2,028
United States	Uzbek, Southern	25,945
Total:	**541 People Groups**	**28,945,173**

This data was provided by the International Mission Board—Global Research, March 2012, http://www.imb.org/globalresearch/ (accessed March 27, 2012 at http://www.grdweb.info/gsec/Overview/tabid/259/Default.aspx).

Appendix 2

Unreached People Groups in the West (Excluding the United States and Canada), Global Research

Country	People Group	Population
Andorra	British	244
Andorra	French	5,333
Andorra	Portuguese	8,381
Andorra	Andorran	34,049
Andorra	Spaniard	24,237
Australia	Arab	300,000
Australia	Deaf Australian	99,927
Australia	Japanese	34,413
Australia	Anglo-New Zealander	160,681
Australia	British	1,038,161
Australia	Irish	50,256
Australia	Irish Traveller	3,563
Australia	Welsh	120,209
Australia	Armenian	16,772
Australia	Estonian	6,888
Australia	Finnish	17,640
Australia	French	43,564
Australia	Austrian	44,053
Australia	Dutch	260,475
Australia	German	681,694
Australia	Greek	306,723
Australia	Hungarian	56,808
Australia	Italian	716,031
Australia	Maltese	61,265
Australia	Portuguese	41,226
Australia	Romani, Balkan	6,500
Australia	Bulgar	3,368
Australia	Croat	78,478
Australia	Macedonian	89,144
Australia	Serb	70,702
Australia	Slovene	13,511
Australia	Czech	17,640
Australia	Pole	72,843
Australia	Slovak	7,141
Australia	Spaniard	16,521
Australia	Jew	125,000
Australia	Malay	21,271
Australia	Thaayoore	366
Australia	Watjari	311
Australia	Kurd, Northern	5,468

Country	People Group	Population
Australia	Afghan	19,400
Australia	Persian	9,568
Australia	Indo-Pakistani	374,032
Australia	Cambodian	25,549
Australia	Thai	30,025
Australia	Burmese	13,800
Australia	Karen	4,200
Australia	Turk	59,402
Austria	Arab	7,236
Austria	Deaf Austrian	39,386
Austria	Belgian	630
Austria	French	15,500
Austria	Austrian	7,475,240
Austria	German	270,000
Austria	Liechtensteiner	580
Austria	Luxembourgeois	334
Austria	Schwyzerdutsch	289,000
Austria	Greek	5,000
Austria	Hungarian	40,583
Austria	Italian	7,855
Austria	Portuguese	202
Austria	Romani, Sinte	500
Austria	Russian	15,500
Austria	Croat	150,719
Austria	Slovene	24,855
Austria	Czech	7,855
Austria	Pole	40,321
Austria	Spaniard	3,927
Austria	Kurd, Northern	23,800
Austria	Persian	16,539
Austria	Turk	72,375
Belgium	Iraqi	2,062
Belgium	Arab, Algerian	3,113
Belgium	Arab, Moroccan	157,200
Belgium	Arab, Tunisian	7,330
Belgium	Kabyle	49,000
Belgium	Shawiya	37,600
Belgium	Deaf Belgian	26,300
Belgium	Han Chinese, Cantonese	500
Belgium	Han Chinese, Mandarin	16,250
Belgium	Kosovar	20,010
Belgium	Tosk	3,355
Belgium	Armenian	5,503
Belgium	Chechen	542
Belgium	Georgian	3,526
Belgium	Flemish	6,050,256

Country	People Group	Population
Belgium	Luxembourgeois	4,300
Belgium	Italian	204,400
Belgium	Portuguese	62,880
Belgium	Moldovan	1,642
Belgium	Romanian	20,620
Belgium	Russian	3,750
Belgium	Serb	2,680
Belgium	Spaniard	43,397
Belgium	Kurd, Northern	26,400
Belgium	Afghan	4,800
Belgium	Persian	3,560
Belgium	Punjabi	50
Belgium	Urdu	9,100
Belgium	Burundi	1,941
Belgium	Guinean	2,716
Belgium	Angolan	5,481
Belgium	Liberian	2,139
Belgium	Kazakh	2,688
Belgium	Turk	51,800
Denmark	Arab	1,500
Denmark	Deaf Danish	24,400
Denmark	Dutch	26,400
Denmark	German	25,900
Denmark	Portuguese	1,000
Denmark	Danish Traveller	3,155
Denmark	Dane	5,086,272
Denmark	Faroese	48,150
Denmark	Icelander	8,440
Denmark	Norwegian	10,166
Denmark	Swede	21,345
Denmark	Russian	1,020
Denmark	Croat	5,400
Denmark	Pole	20,000
Denmark	Spaniard	5,400
Denmark	Greenlander	10,000
Denmark	Persian	9,000
Denmark	Punjabi	1,000
Denmark	Urdu	3,150
Denmark	Turk	30,500
Finland	Deaf Finn	8,000
Finland	Finnish	4,868,194
Finland	Karelian	11,000
Finland	Finnish Lapp	5,730
Finland	Swede	312,558
Finland	Russian	45,300
France	Saharawl	25,000

Country	People Group	Population
France	Arab, Iraqi	25,000
France	Arab, Jordanian	25,000
France	Arab, Lebanese	25,000
France	Arab, Palestinian	25,000
France	Arab, Syrian	53,600
France	Druze	25,000
France	Arab, Algerian	800,000
France	Arab, Moroccan	524,686
France	Arab, Tunisian	250,000
France	Berber, Jaballa	25,000
France	Arab, Sudanese	300
France	Assyrian	3,700
France	Kabyle	537,000
France	Berber, Riffi	117,000
France	Mzab	25,000
France	Shawiya	114,000
France	Berber, Ishilhayn	150,000
France	Berber, Middle Atlas	114,000
France	Arab, Egyptian	25,000
France	Ibidites	25,000
France	Deaf French	168,690
France	Han Chinese	171,660
France	Han Chinese, Min Nan	1,000
France	Japanese	11,600
France	Tosk	100
France	Armenian	461,000
France	Lithuanian	100
France	Basque, Navarro-Labourdin	898,800
France	Georgian	2,500
France	Breton	685,000
France	Corsican	308,744
France	French	35,143,929
France	Gascon	432,000
France	Languedocien	2,469,954
France	Limousin	717,600
France	Picard	1,900,833
France	Provencal-Alpin	2,840,400
France	Provencal-Vaudois	70,000
France	Walloon	61,749
France	Alsatian	1,660,242
France	Dutch	84,200
France	German Swiss	37,050
France	Luxembourgeois	41,636
France	Hungarian	100
France	Italian	1,162,878
France	Portuguese	926,200

Country	People Group	Population
France	Romanian	14,300
France	Arliski Balkan Romany	10,500
France	Black Gypsy	1,000
France	Romani, Balkan	12,000
France	Romani, Sinte	10,000
France	Romani, Vlax	12,000
France	Dane	13,000
France	Swede	13,000
France	Russian	124,000
France	Ukrainian	22,000
France	Bosnian	100
France	Croat	20,000
France	Serb	25,000
France	Czech	13,000
France	Pole	208,600
France	Catalonian	303,500
France	Spaniard	740,987
France	Jew	600,000
France	Malagasy	61,749
France	Singaporean	100
France	Kurd, Northern	74,000
France	Afghan	37,050
France	Persian	61,800
France	Bengali	30,600
France	Gujarati	1,040
France	Hindi	100
France	Maldivian	100
France	Sikh	10,850
France	Tamil	100,000
France	Urdu	100
France	Lao	18,500
France	Khmer	100,000
France	Black Tai	1,000
France	Thai	10,354
France	Vietnamese	617,488
France	Mandyak	22,000
France	Jola-Fogny	100
France	Comorian	93,700
France	Fulbe Jeeri	900
France	Fulfulde-Fulani	30,874
France	Pulaar	1,000
France	Nigerian	100
France	Mandinka	100
France	Malian	300
France	Mauritian	100
France	Reunionese	12,350

Country	People Group	Population
France	Ivorian	800
France	Sierra Leonean	100
France	West Africans, French-Speaking	124,609
France	Turk	222,297
Germany	Arab	5,000
Germany	Arab, Middle Eastern	62,000
Germany	Arab, Syrian	1,695
Germany	Iraqi	5,000
Germany	Arab, Moroccan	46,100
Germany	Arab, Tunisian	26,300
Germany	Chaldean, Neo-aramaic	3,000
Germany	Turoyo	20,200
Germany	Deaf German	395,374
Germany	Han Chinese	50,885
Germany	Japanese	24,500
Germany	Mongolian	1,538
Germany	Tosk	32,921
Germany	British	100,027
Germany	Armenian	33,660
Germany	Latvian	9,150
Germany	Lithuanian	23,522
Germany	Chechen	1,000
Germany	Bavarian	245,119
Germany	Dutch	136,274
Germany	Eastern Frisian	11,350
Germany	German	56,775,095
Germany	German Swiss	37,197
Germany	Lower Saxons	4,500
Germany	Luxembourgeois	12,231
Germany	Mainfrankisch	4,902,380
Germany	Northern Frisian	4,900
Germany	Rommane Gypsy	32,680
Germany	Swabian	817,064
Germany	Upper Saxons	2,000,000
Germany	Italian	817,000
Germany	Portuguese	113,208
Germany	Romani, Vlax	12,000
Germany	Dane	51,630
Germany	Belarussian	9,241
Germany	Ukrainian	124,293
Germany	Bosnian	286,000
Germany	Bulgarian	4,100
Germany	Croat	322,896
Germany	Macedonian	3,865
Germany	Serb	490,200
Germany	Slovene	20,034

Country	People Group	Population
Germany	Northern Sorb	7,222
Germany	Pole	326,835
Germany	Upper Sorbian	18,200
Germany	Ethiopian	5,778
Germany	Jew	122,500
Germany	Jew, Russian	300,000
Germany	Kurd, Northern	540,000
Germany	Afghan	72,200
Germany	Persian	98,050
Germany	Bengali	683
Germany	Bhojpuri	17,000
Germany	Hindi	25,560
Germany	Tamil	60,000
Germany	Urdu	17,500
Germany	Khmer	12,751
Germany	Thai	20,588
Germany	Vietnamese	83,446
Germany	Ghanaian	40,000
Germany	Eritrean	1,800
Germany	Azeri	100
Germany	Kazakh	5,000
Germany	Turk	2,206,100
Greenland	Dane	3,381
Iceland	Deaf Icelander	1,384
Iceland	Dane	2,977
Iceland	Icelander	324,290
Iceland	Norwegian	976
Ireland	Deaf Irish	20,662
Ireland	Irish	4,278,407
Ireland	Irish Traveller	6,030
Ireland	Romanian	8,667
Ireland	Russian	2,102
Ireland	Bosnian	1,600
Ireland	Pole	120,000
Ireland	Spaniard	3,983
Ireland	Urdu	2,299
Ireland	Nigerian	4,552
Italy	Iraqi	2,551
Italy	Arab, Libyan	1,466
Italy	Arab, Algerian	15,493
Italy	Arab, Moroccan	253,362
Italy	Arab, Tunisian	68,630
Italy	Arab, Sudanese	746
Italy	Shawiya	37,000
Italy	Arab, Egyptian	40,583
Italy	Deaf Italian	278,400

Country	People Group	Population
Italy	Han Chinese	100,109
Italy	Albanian	402,000
Italy	Arbereshe	80,000
Italy	Armenian	2,600
Italy	Franco-Provencal	70,000
Italy	French	28,400
Italy	Bavarian Austrian	258,885
Italy	Cimbrian	2,230
Italy	German	225,000
Italy	Mocheno	1,900
Italy	Walser	3,400
Italy	Greek	14,330
Italy	Campidanese Sardinian	923,281
Italy	Dolomite	30,000
Italy	Italian	37,788,545
Italy	Nuorese	269,422
Italy	Rhaeto-Romansh	21,000
Italy	Sassarese Sardinian	459,185
Italy	Sicilian	5,087,794
Italy	Maltese	28,000
Italy	Romani, Balkan	5,100
Italy	Romani, Sinte	14,000
Italy	Romani, Vlax	4,000
Italy	Russian	34,396
Italy	Bosnian	29,000
Italy	Pomak	2,100
Italy	Slovene	52,000
Italy	Catalan	20,000
Italy	Spaniard	11,062
Italy	Somali	6,440
Italy	Filipino	77,025
Italy	Kurd, Northern	3,500
Italy	Afghan	2,000
Italy	Persian	1,000
Italy	Bangladeshi	30,000
Italy	Sri Lanken	1,500
Italy	Wolof	2,000
Italy	Nigerian	9,621
Italy	Liberian	500
Liechtenstein	German	1,346
Liechtenstein	German Swiss	3,658
Liechtenstein	Italian	1,171
Luxembourg	Deaf Luxembourger	2,081
Luxembourg	British	6,898
Luxembourg	French	22,290
Luxembourg	Walloon	3,908

Country	People Group	Population
Luxembourg	Dutch	4,395
Luxembourg	German	11,215
Luxembourg	Luxembourgeois	309,324
Luxembourg	Italian	21,193
Luxembourg	Portuguese	65,442
Luxembourg	Spaniard	2,417
Malta	Arab	7,200
Malta	Deaf Maltese	1,960
Malta	British	25,681
Malta	Italian	5,000
Malta	Maltese	397,222
Monaco	French	14,796
Monaco	Provencal	4,500
Monaco	Italian	5,094
Monaco	Ligurian	6,596
Monaco	Portuguese	600
Monaco	Spaniard	300
Netherlands	Arab, Lebanese	2,162
Netherlands	Arab, Levantine	2,817
Netherlands	Arab, Algerian	69,658
Netherlands	Arab, Moroccan	114,947
Netherlands	Arab, Tunisian	69,658
Netherlands	Arab, Sudanese	1,387
Netherlands	Chaldean, Neo-aramaic	1,116
Netherlands	Turoyo	4,644
Netherlands	Berber	278,917
Netherlands	Deaf Dutch	84,435
Netherlands	Han Chinese	91,050
Netherlands	Korean	6,994
Netherlands	Frisian	334,701
Netherlands	German	111,567
Netherlands	Lower Saxons	1,707,140
Netherlands	Romani, Sinte	569
Netherlands	Romani, Vlax	1,138
Netherlands	Russian	4,930
Netherlands	Croat	4,463
Netherlands	Spaniard	19,100
Netherlands	Eritrean	2,049
Netherlands	Somali	1,726
Netherlands	Jew, Portuguese	17,071
Netherlands	Antillean Creole	139,494
Netherlands	Surinamese Creole	345,436
Netherlands	Caribbean Javanese	8,621
Netherlands	Indonesian	115,000
Netherlands	Surinamese Aucan	27,892
Netherlands	Kurd, Northern	45,524

Country	People Group	Population
Netherlands	Afghan	29,297
Netherlands	Persian	8,925
Netherlands	East Indian	124,143
Netherlands	Tamil	7,888
Netherlands	Guinea	3,091
Netherlands	Nigerian	5,578
Netherlands	Angolan	7,461
Netherlands	Crioulo, Upper Guinea	13,794
Netherlands	Liberian	2,410
Netherlands	Sierra Leonean	2,453
Netherlands	Azeri	113
Netherlands	Turk	360,133
New Zealand	Deaf New Zealander	19,888
New Zealand	Anglo-Australian	26,355
New Zealand	Anglo-Canadian	5,604
New Zealand	British (English)	44,202
New Zealand	British (Scottish)	15,039
New Zealand	Irish	12,651
New Zealand	Welsh	3,771
New Zealand	Austrian	1,092
New Zealand	Dutch	28,641
New Zealand	German	10,917
New Zealand	Greek	2,355
New Zealand	Hungarian	1,212
New Zealand	Italian	3,117
New Zealand	Romanian	1,704
New Zealand	Danish	1,932
New Zealand	Russian	4,833
New Zealand	Croat	2,547
New Zealand	Serb	1,029
New Zealand	Slovene	1,640
New Zealand	Pole	3,690
New Zealand	Jew	6,969
Norway	Deaf Norwegian	21,927
Norway	Finn	12,300
Norway	Arctic Lapp	60,000
Norway	Lule Saami	500
Norway	Northern Saami	15,000
Norway	Southern Saami	300
Norway	Romani, Vlax	500
Norway	Tattare Gypsy	6,000
Norway	Dane	12,000
Norway	Swede	21,000
Norway	Spaniard	851
Portugal	Arab, Levantine	21,000
Portugal	Arab, Moroccan	6,300

Country	People Group	Population
Portugal	Deaf Portuguese	50,717
Portugal	Han Chinese, Mandarin	2,477
Portugal	Japanese	757
Portugal	Belgian	1,766
Portugal	French	5,804
Portugal	Austrian	449
Portugal	Luxembourgeois	64
Portugal	Greek	107
Portugal	Italian	2,371
Portugal	Mirandesa	10,000
Portugal	Portuguese	10,710,145
Portugal	Black Gypsy	5,400
Portugal	Romani, Vlax	500
Portugal	Spanish Calo	5,000
Portugal	Galician	15,000
Portugal	Spaniard	42,000
Portugal	Timorese	3,100
Portugal	Indian	1,116
Portugal	Angolan	80,000
Portugal	Caboverdian Mestico	35,000
San Marino	Emiliano-Romagnolo	22,889
San Marino	Italian	5,230
Spain	Arab, Syrian	25
Spain	Libyan	100
Spain	Arab, Algerian	5,000
Spain	Arab, Moroccan	500,000
Spain	North Africans, Canary Islands	28,300
Spain	Arab, Egyptian	500
Spain	Deaf Spanish	193,637
Spain	Han Chinese, Mandarin	170,000
Spain	Japanese	500
Spain	Basque	2,304,000
Spain	Gascon	3,814
Spain	Dutch	8,000
Spain	German	190,584
Spain	Portuguese	140,424
Spain	Romanian	796,576
Spain	Norwegian	10,000
Spain	Russian	922
Spain	Bulgarian	164,353
Spain	Pole	84,823
Spain	Aragonese	1,988,000
Spain	Asturian	862,998
Spain	Catalan	7,512,381
Spain	Extremaduran	1,086,373
Spain	Fala	10,500

Country	People Group	Population
Spain	Galician	3,173,400
Spain	Spaniard	25,563,695
Spain	Valenciano	2,500,000
Spain	Jew, Spanish	800
Spain	Brazilian	33,290
Spain	Filipino	38,634
Spain	Persian	100
Spain	Indian	100
Spain	Pakistani	100
Spain	Senegalese	2,000
Spain	Guinean	1,000
Spain	Nigerian	5,111
Spain	Caboverdian Mestico	1,000
Sweden	Arab, Levantine	8,500
Sweden	Assyrian	9,500
Sweden	Deaf Swedish	40,192
Sweden	Latvian	3,635
Sweden	Estonian	16,635
Sweden	Finn	352,687
Sweden	Ingrian-Finn	300
Sweden	Lule Saami	1,500
Sweden	Northern Saami	4,000
Sweden	Southern Saami	400
Sweden	Dutch	8,824
Sweden	German Swiss	3,244
Sweden	Hungarian	27,582
Sweden	Black Gypsy	1,592
Sweden	Romani, Vlax	2,500
Sweden	Swedish Traveller	25,000
Sweden	Tattare Gypsy	25,000
Sweden	Dane	9,854
Sweden	Norwegian	4,293
Sweden	Russian	18,937
Sweden	Croat	13,731
Sweden	Slovene	1,413
Sweden	Czech	6,453
Sweden	Pole	93,198
Sweden	Slovak	4,071
Sweden	Chilean	28,704
Sweden	Tibetan	900
Sweden	Turk	5,100
Switzerland	Arab	2,874
Switzerland	Deaf Swiss	38,540
Switzerland	Han Chinese	1,494
Switzerland	Franco-Provencal	7,967
Switzerland	Dutch	14,943

Country	People Group	Population
Switzerland	German	268,592
Switzerland	Swiss (Alemannisch)	4,296,315
Switzerland	Hungarian	14,943
Switzerland	Italian	820,697
Switzerland	Lombard	344,842
Switzerland	Portuguese	216,873
Switzerland	Romani, Sinte	23,900
Switzerland	Swede	2,299
Switzerland	Czech	7,127
Switzerland	Spaniard	91,954
Switzerland	Jew	1,494
Switzerland	Italo-Swiss	267,742
Switzerland	Turk	91,764
United Kingdom	Arab, Middle Eastern	500,000
United Kingdom	Arab, Moroccan	5,786
United Kingdom	Assyrian, Turoyo	8,236
United Kingdom	Assyrian, Neo-Aramaic	5,000
United Kingdom	Berber	2,893
United Kingdom	Arab, Egyptian	45,000
United Kingdom	Deaf British	290,117
United Kingdom	Han Chinese	312,000
United Kingdom	Korean	12,000
United Kingdom	Khalka Mongol	8,100
United Kingdom	Tosk	30,000
United Kingdom	Cornish	2,000
United Kingdom	Irish Traveller	5,800
United Kingdom	Scottish Traveller	4,000
United Kingdom	Armenian	29,415
United Kingdom	Latvian	12,000
United Kingdom	Estonian	2,005
United Kingdom	Finn	11,322
United Kingdom	French	96,281
United Kingdom	Afrikaner	29,000
United Kingdom	Dutch	40,438
United Kingdom	German Swiss	13,000
United Kingdom	Greek	200,000
United Kingdom	Greek Cypriot	208,400
United Kingdom	Hungarian	19,000
United Kingdom	Italian	200,000
United Kingdom	Portuguese	17,000
United Kingdom	Romanian	41,000
United Kingdom	Anglo-Romani Gypsy	90,000
United Kingdom	Romani, Vlax	4,100
United Kingdom	Traveller Gypsy	70,000
United Kingdom	Dane	18,695
United Kingdom	Norwegian	13,798

Country	People Group	Population
United Kingdom	Swede	22,525
United Kingdom	Belarussian	4,900
United Kingdom	Russian	74,000
United Kingdom	Ukrainian	69,000
United Kingdom	Bosnian	2,000
United Kingdom	Serb	31,244
United Kingdom	Czech	12,220
United Kingdom	Pole	750,000
United Kingdom	Spaniard	43,010
United Kingdom	Eritrean	14,708
United Kingdom	Somali	150,000
United Kingdom	Arab, Judeo-Iraqi	4,000
United Kingdom	Hasidim	433,977
United Kingdom	Jew	323,000
United Kingdom	Malaysian Malay	47,652
United Kingdom	Kurd, Northern	100,000
United Kingdom	Afghan	10,500
United Kingdom	Parsee	75,000
United Kingdom	Southern Pashto	87,400
United Kingdom	Persian	29,415
United Kingdom	Bengali	366,565
United Kingdom	Gujarati	140,000
United Kingdom	Hindi	465,000
United Kingdom	Kashmiri-Punjabi	117,660
United Kingdom	Goan	10,589
United Kingdom	Punjabi, Eastern	470,641
United Kingdom	Punjabi, Western	102,560
United Kingdom	Sindhi	30,000
United Kingdom	Pakistani	376,850
United Kingdom	Urdu	176,490
United Kingdom	Khmer	10,000
United Kingdom	Vietnamese	100,000
United Kingdom	Akan	17,000
United Kingdom	Nigerian	42,220
United Kingdom	Mauritian	22,355
United Kingdom	Seychellese Creole	2,353
United Kingdom	Sierra Leonean	4,100
United Kingdom	Burmese	12,354
United Kingdom	Turk	60,000
United Kingdom	Turkish Cypriot	161,300
TOTAL:	**632 People Groups**	**290,134,912**

This data was provided by the International Mission Board—Global Research, March 2012, www.imb.org/globalresearch/ (accessed March 29, 2012, at www.grdweb.info/gsec/Overview/tabid/259/Default.aspx).

Appendix 3

Unreached People Groups in the West (Joshua Project)

Country	People Group Name in Country	Population
Andorra	Arab, Moroccan	600
Andorra	Indo-Pakistani	480
Andorra	Jew	210
Australia	Mandaean	3,680
Australia	Arab	61,900
Australia	Cocos Islander, Kukus	1,150
Australia	Japanese	34,600
Australia	Malay	790
Australia	Thai, Central	28,600
Australia	Turk	57,600
Australia	Khmer, Central	27,300
Australia	Jew	108,000
Australia	Kurd, Kurmanji	17,200
Australia	Persian	90,800
Austria	Afghan	32,100
Austria	Indo-Pakistani	21,800
Austria	Jew, German	9,000
Austria	Kurd, Kurmanji	23,800
Austria	Persian	16,600
Austria	Turk	156,000
Belgium	Arab, Libyan	4,300
Belgium	Jew	30,300
Belgium	South Asian	9,360
Belgium	Algerian, Arabic-speaking	25,800
Belgium	Kurd, Kurmanji	27,000
Belgium	Arab, Moroccan	161,000
Belgium	Shawiya	38,600
Belgium	Arab, Tunisian	7,530
Belgium	Turk	64,500
Belgium	Persian	3,650
Canada	Albanian, Kosovars	1,130
Canada	Arab, Jordanian	4,510
Canada	Arab, Kuwait	960
Canada	Arab, Northern Yemeni	1,160
Canada	Arab, Shuwa, Baggara	660
Canada	Arab, Tunisian	6,470
Canada	Dungan	70
Canada	Fulfulde, Fulani	570
Canada	Jew, English Speaking	141,000
Canada	Mongol, Khalka	1,080
Canada	North African	43,100

Country	People Group Name in Country	Population
Canada	Parsee	27,200
Canada	Pashtun, Southern	44,200
Canada	Tatar	620
Canada	Tigre, Eritrean	330
Canada	Arab, Saudi - Najdi	1,590
Canada	Bengali	38,500
Canada	Hindi	252,000
Canada	Jew, Israeli	72,100
Canada	Japanese	59,500
Canada	Jew, Eastern Yiddish-speaking	54,100
Canada	Khmer, Central	710
Canada	Malay	92,400
Canada	Punjabi	866,000
Canada	Sinhalese	3,980
Canada	Thai, Central	4,430
Canada	Turk	24,600
Canada	Azerbaijani, North	1,570
Canada	Bosniak	15,700
Canada	Kurd, Kurmanji	6,870
Canada	Berber, Kabyle	9,950
Canada	Somali	36,700
Canada	Algerian, Arabic-speaking	21,000
Canada	Arab, Libyan	1,920
Canada	Arab, Moroccan	29,900
Canada	Arab, Sudanese	10,600
Canada	Arab, Iraqi	23,400
Canada	Gujarati	1,730
Canada	Burmese	2,230
Canada	Wolof	1,840
Canada	Bambara	650
Denmark	Arab, Iraqi	12,700
Denmark	Bosniak	24,000
Denmark	Chinese	5,200
Denmark	Jew, Danish	6,400
Denmark	Kurd, Kurmanji	11,000
Denmark	Pashtun, Northern	11,700
Denmark	Persian	14,800
Denmark	Punjabi	1,040
Denmark	Somali	16,200
Denmark	Thai, Central	7,500
Denmark	Turk	90,200
Denmark	Urdu	3,220
Finland	Arab, Iraqi	8,140
Finland	Jew, Finnish	1,140
Finland	Kurd, Kurmanji	6,100
Finland	Somali	9,970

Country	People Group Name in Country	Population
Finland	Tatar	810
Finland	Thai, Central	4,070
Finland	Turk	4,170
France	Bambara	44,000
France	Cham, Western, Tjam	1,090
France	Giay, Nhang	100
France	Maninka	62,900
France	Pashtun, Northern	37,800
France	Soninke, Sarakole	9,440
France	Tay	1,890
France	Tuareg	25,200
France	Wolof	39,500
France	Bengali	31,200
France	Comorian, other	94,500
France	Gujarati	1,060
France	Hmong, White	10,900
France	Iu Mien	2,180
France	Japanese	12,100
France	Khmer, Central	69,200
France	Lao	18,900
France	Turk	227,000
France	Algerian, Arabic-speaking	1,258,000
France	Berber, Kabyle	692,000
France	Kurd, Kurmanji	81,800
France	Berber, Imazighen	157,000
France	Arab, Moroccan	631,000
France	Berber, Riffian	126,000
France	Moor	18,900
France	Shawiya	189,000
France	Arab, Tunisian	211,000
France	Han Chinese, Mandarin	37,800
France	Tukulor, Pulaar	100
France	Persian	62,900
France	Jola-Fonyi, Diola	100
France	Fulani	31,500
France	Jew, French	484,000
France	Khmu	520
Germany	Adyghe, Kabardian	2,090
Germany	Algerian, Arabic-speaking	228,000
Germany	Jew, Western Yiddish-speaking	49,300
Germany	Pashtun, Northern	32,500
Germany	Punjabi	16,300
Germany	Shawiya	36,800
Germany	Zaza-Alevica	5,000
Germany	Bhojpuri Bihari	16,900
Germany	Chechen	990

Country	People Group Name in Country	Population
Germany	Jew, German	70,000
Germany	Kazakh	40,800
Germany	Kurd, Kurmanji	537,000
Germany	Persian	97,600
Germany	Turk	2,301,000
Germany	Urdu	17,500
Germany	Japanese	24,400
Germany	Bosniak	285,000
Germany	Arab, Tunisian	26,200
Germany	Arab, Moroccan	45,900
Iceland	Thai, Northeastern	570
Ireland	Hindi	8,110
Ireland	Jew	1,200
Ireland	Turks	2,270
Ireland	Urdu	7,240
Italy	Arab, North African	1,216,000
Italy	Bengali, Bangladeshi	50,000
Italy	Bosniak	3,590
Italy	Japanese	600
Italy	Jew, Italian	28,400
Italy	Kurd, Kurmanji	12,000
Italy	Mocheno	2,030
Italy	Persian	1,050
Italy	Pomak	2,390
Italy	Shawiya	38,700
Italy	Somali	52,600
Italy	Turks	27,300
Liechtenstein	Jew, German	50
Liechtenstein	Turks	1,060
Luxembourg	Jew, German	600
Luxembourg	Turks	710
Malta	Indo-Pakistani	60
Malta	Jew, Maltese	60
Malta	Turks	760
Monaco	Jew, French	590
Netherlands	Berber, Rifi	153,000
Netherlands	Jew, Dutch	30,500
Netherlands	Yugoslav former, generic	13,200
Netherlands	Azerbaijani, North	100
Netherlands	Algerian, Arabic-speaking	87,500
Netherlands	Sarnami Hindi, East Indian	116,000
Netherlands	Kurd, Kurmanji	71,700
Netherlands	Arab, Moroccan	348,000
Netherlands	Somali	15,300
Netherlands	Arab, Sudanese	1,330
Netherlands	Arab, Tunisian	83,300

Country	People Group Name in Country	Population
Netherlands	Turk	385,000
Netherlands	Persian	30,000
New Zealand	Isan, Northeastern Thai	5,230
New Zealand	Jew	7,500
New Zealand	Khmer, Central	7,590
New Zealand	Malay	2,360
New Zealand	Somali	2,160
New Zealand	Turks	1,590
Norway	Arab, Middle East	7,330
Norway	Bosniak	15,400
Norway	Indian	7,450
Norway	Jew, Norwegian	1,200
Norway	Kurd, Kurmanji	4,850
Norway	Pashtun, Southern	6,810
Norway	Persian	15,000
Norway	Punjabi	7,430
Norway	Sinhalese	13,100
Norway	Somali	18,800
Norway	Thai, Northeastern	8,110
Norway	Tigre, Eritrean	2,760
Norway	Turk	14,700
Norway	Urdu	28,800
Portugal	Arab, Maghrebi	6,160
Portugal	Japanese	770
Portugal	Jew, Portuguese	510
Portugal	Kurd, Kurmanji	150
Portugal	Turks	760
Spain	Arab, Lebanese	64,500
Spain	Arab, Maghrebi	604,000
Spain	Japanese	2,150
Spain	Jew	11,000
Spain	Jew, Spanish	940
Spain	Kurd, Kurmanji	860
Spain	Turks	4,490
Sweden	Arab, Moroccan	5,670
Sweden	Bosniak	66,100
Sweden	Jew, Swedish	15,000
Sweden	Kurd, Kurmanji	10,500
Sweden	Mandaean	5,080
Sweden	Somali	16,100
Sweden	Tibetan	920
Sweden	Turk	24,500
Switzerland	Bosniak	142,000
Switzerland	Jew, French	17,600
Switzerland	Kurd, Kurmanji	7,720
Switzerland	Thai, Central	7,760

Country	People Group Name in Country	Population
Switzerland	Tibetan, Zhongdian	320
Switzerland	Turk	45,600
United Kingdom	Arab, Yemeni	31,400
United Kingdom	Berber, Kabyle	3,130
United Kingdom	Mandaean	1,010
United Kingdom	Sylhetti Bengali	113,000
United Kingdom	Turk	56,000
United Kingdom	Yahudic, Judeo-Iraqi	6,270
United Kingdom	Bengali, Bangla-Bhasa	375,000
United Kingdom	Berber, Imazighen	2,930
United Kingdom	Burmese	13,200
United Kingdom	Tigre, Eritrean	15,700
United Kingdom	Gujarati	314,000
United Kingdom	Hindi	485,000
United Kingdom	Persian	80,300
United Kingdom	Jew	292,000
United Kingdom	Kurd, Kurmanji	25,100
United Kingdom	Malay, Malaysian	50,800
United Kingdom	Arab, Moroccan	31,400
United Kingdom	Pashtun, Southern	94,100
United Kingdom	Punjabi	593,000
United Kingdom	Sindhi	27,000
United Kingdom	Somali	93,600
United Kingdom	Cypriots, Turkish	32,000
United Kingdom	Urdu	188,000
United Kingdom	Kashmiri	125,000
United Kingdom	Punjabi, Western	250,000
United Kingdom	Parsee	87,800
United Kingdom	Pashtun, Northern	94,100
United States	Adyghe	3,310
United States	Adyghe, Kabardian	3,580
United States	Algerian, Arabic-speaking	23,900
United States	Arab, Najdi	5,590
United States	Arab, Saudi - Hijazi	5,590
United States	Arab, Sudanese	1,240
United States	Arab, Yemeni	5,010
United States	Arapaho	9,140
United States	Assamese	190
United States	Azerbaijani, North	160
United States	Baggara, Arab, Shuwa	2,240
United States	Balkar	570
United States	Bengali	213,000
United States	Berber, Imazighen	130
United States	Bisaya, Sabah Bisaya	13,500
United States	Bosniak	110,000
United States	Brao	100

Country	People Group Name in Country	Population
United States	Burmese, Myen	18,000
United States	Cham, Western	3,120
United States	Chitimacha	330
United States	Chumash	3,500
United States	Fulani, Western	11,700
United States	Gujar	243,000
United States	Hkun, Khuen	2,640
United States	Indonesian	47,000
United States	Iu Mien	16,900
United States	Jew	4,853,000
United States	Jew, Bukharic	52,000
United States	Jew, Eastern Yiddish-speaking	187,000
United States	Jew, Israeli	203,000
United States	Jew, Russian	386,000
United States	Jew, Spanish	150
United States	Jew, Spanish-speaking	14,700
United States	Kalmyk-Oirat, Western Mongul	930
United States	Kashaya	50
United States	Kashmiri Muslim	220
United States	Khamet, Lamet	90
United States	Khmer, Cambodian	188,000
United States	Khmu	2,210
United States	Kurd, Kurmanji	49,700
United States	Kurd, Sorani	8,570
United States	Lao, Laotian Tai	155,000
United States	Laven, Boloven	34,100
United States	Malay	8,260
United States	Maldivian	30
United States	Mandaean	1,770
United States	Maninke	11,400
United States	Marathi	33,700
United States	Mon, Talaing	390
United States	Mongol	1,410
United States	Nepalese	8,380
United States	Okinawan, Ryukuan	13,300
United States	Oriya	1,080
United States	Panamint	100
United States	Parsee	78,000
United States	Pashtun, Northern	48,500
United States	Phu Thai	52,700
United States	Sindhi	5,680
United States	Sinhalese	11,500
United States	Somali	78,300
United States	Tai Dam, Black Tai	4,040
United States	Tai Lue	4,260
United States	Tajik	140

Country	People Group Name in Country	Population
United States	Tatar	10,400
United States	Tay	620
United States	Thai, Central	140,000
United States	Tibetan, Central	4,560
United States	Tuareg, Algerian	50
United States	Turk	364,000
United States	Urdu	286,000
United States	Uyghur	950
United States	Uzbek, Northern	24,900
TOTAL:	**329 Unreached People Groups**	**27,332,120**

Data taken from: Joshua Project, www.joshuaproject.net (accessed March 29, 2012).

Notes

Introduction

[1]The information regarding the Chos was taken from "Five hundred come to Christ and two churches start as a result of Nepal/India mission trip" by Sharon Mager, *Baptist Life*, August 2009, http://www.baptistlifeonline.org/2009/08/five-hundred-come-to-christ-and-two-churches-start-as-a-result-of-nepalindia-mission-trip (accessed August 17, 2009).

[2]Frank Obien with Al Janssen, *Building Bridges of Love: A Handbook for Sharing God's Love with International Students* (San Bernardino, CA: Campus Crusade for Christ, 1974), 21.

[3]Don Bjork, "Foreign Missions: Next Door and Down the Street," *Christianity Today* 29, no. 10 (1985): 20.

[4]Philip Jenkins, *The Next Christendom: The Coming of Global Christianity* (New York: Oxford University Press, 2007).

Chapter 1: Immigration, Migration, and Kingdom Perspective

[1]Adapted from the pamphlet *Praying for the International People Groups of Louisville, Kentucky: A Guide,* produced by the Kentucky Baptist Convention.

[2]Russell King, ed., *The History of Human Migration* (London: New Holland Publishers, 2007), 8.

[3]Ibid.

[4]UNHCR, "Refugees," http://www.unhcr.org/pages/49c3646c125.html (accessed August 21, 2009).

[5]UNHCR, "Asylum-Seekers," http://www.unhcr.org/pages/49c3646c137.html (accessed August 21, 2009).

[6]Stephen Castles and Mark J. Miller, *The Age of Migration: International Population Movements in the Modern World,* 4th ed. (New York: The Guilford Press, 2009), xviii.

[7]Ibid., 5.

[8]For discussions related to the challenges of interpreting these verses, see Stephen G. Wilson, *The Gentiles and the Gentile Mission in Luke–Acts* (Cambridge: Cambridge University Press, 2005) and John B. Polhill, *Acts,* The New American Commentary, vol. 26 (Nashville, TN: Broadman Press, 1992), 373-75.

Chapter 2: What in the World Is God Doing?

[1]"Citizenship," http://www.homeoffice.gov.uk/publications/science-research-statistics/research-statistics/immigration-asylum-research/immigration-brief-q3-2011/citizenship (accessed March 26, 2012).

[2]Alan Travis, "Figures Show 20% Increase in Net Migration to UK," *Guardian* 26, August 2010, http://www.guardian.co.uk/uk/2010/aug/26/net-migration-to-uk-increases (accessed August 31, 2010).

[3]Phillip and Kandace Connor, *Who Is My Neighbor? Reaching Internationals in North America* (Princeton, NJ: n.p., 2008), 44, 45, 48, 49. This book is available from www.reachinternationals.com.

[4]United Nations Department of Economic and Social Affairs, *Trends in International Migrant Stock: The 2008 Revision,* 1-3, http://www.un.org/esa/population/migration/UN_MigStock_2008.pdf (accessed February 15, 2011).

[5]United Nations Department of Economic and Social Affairs, Population Division, *International Migration Report 2006: A Global Assessment,* 2009, xv, http://www.un.org/esa/population/publications/2006_MigrationRep/exec_sum.pdf (accessed August 20, 2009).

[6]OECD, *International Migration Outlook: SOPEMI 2010 Edition,* 21, http://www.nbbmuseum.be/doc/seminar2010/nl/bibliografie/kansengroepen/sopemi2010.pdf (accessed February 28, 2011).

[7]"International Migrant Stock: The 2008 Revision" website, United Nations Department of Economic and Social Affairs, Population Division, http://esa.un.org/migration/index.asp (accessed February 15, 2011).

[8]Alain Bélanger and Éric Caron Malenfant, "Ethnocultural Diversity in Canada: Prospects for 2017," *Canadian Social Trends* (Winter 2005): 19, http://www.statcan.gc.ca/pub/11-008-x/2005003/article/8968-eng.pdf (accessed January 25, 2011).

[9]*International Migration Report* 2006, xvi.

[10]*International Migrant Stock: The 2008 Revision* website.

[11]*International Migration Report 2006: A Global Assessment,* "Part One: International Migration Levels, Trends and Policies," 1, http://www.un.org/esa/population/publications/2006_MigrationRep/part_one.pdf (accessed August 20, 2009).

[12]Statistics Canada, *Census snapshot—Immigration in Canada: A Portrait of the Foreign-Born Population, 2006 Census* (catalogue number 11-008-X), 46, http://www.statcan.gc.ca/pub/11-008-x/2008001/article/10556-eng.pdf (accessed August 27, 2009).

[13]Ibid.

[14]Ibid., 48.

[15]Ibid., 50-51.

[16]Ibid., 51-52.

[17]Statistics Canada, "Ethnic Diversity and Immigration," www41.statcan.ca/2007/30000/ceb30000_000_e.htm (accessed June 2, 2009).

[18]*International Migrant Stock: The 2008 Revision* website.

[19]Stephen Castles and Mark J. Miller, *The Age of Migration: International Population Movements in the Modern World,* 4th ed. (New York: The Guilford Press, 2009), 129.

[20]Randall Monger and James Yankay, "U. S. Legal Permanent Residents: 2010," 4, U.S. Department of Homeland Security, http://www.dhs.gov/xlibrary/assets/statistics/publications/lpr_fr_2010.pdf (accessed March 26, 2012).

[21]Daniel C. Martin and Michael Hoefer, "Refugees and Asylees: 2008," *Annual Flow Report,* 3, U.S. Department of Homeland Security, June 2009, http://www.dhs.gov/xlibrary/assets/statistics/publications/ois_rfa_fr_2008.pdf (accessed August 27, 2009).

[22]Daniel C. Martin, "Refugees and Asylees: 2010," 3, U.S. Department of Homeland Security, http://www.dhs.gov/xlibrary/assets/statistics/publications/ois_rfa_fr_2010.pdf (accessed March 26, 2012).

[23]Institute of International Education, "Open Doors 2011—Fast Facts," http://www.iie.org/en/Research-and-Publications/Open-Doors/Data/~/media/Files/Corporate/

Open-Doors/Fast-Facts/Fast%20Facts%202011.ashx (accessed March 26, 2012).
[24]Jan A. B. Jongeneel, "The Mission of Migrant Churches in Europe," *Missiology* 31 (January 2003): 30.
[25]*International Migrant Stock: The 2008 Revision* website.
[26]OECD, *International Migration Outlook: SOPEMI—2008 Edition*, 3, http://www .oecd.org/dataoecd/30/13/41275373.pdf (accessed August 27, 2009).
[27]http://www.migrationinformation.org/feature/display.cfm?id=736 (accessed August 20, 2009).
[28]Philip Danzlman, "British Citizenship Statistics United Kingdom, 2009," *Home Office Statistical Bulletin* (May 27, 2010), 1, http://www.homeoffice.gov.uk/ publications/science-research-statistics/research-statistics/immigration-asylum-research/hosb0910/hosb0910?view=Binary.
[29]Ibid., 11.
[30]Castles and Miller, *The Age of Migration*, 111.
[31]*International Migration Outlook: SOPEMI—2010 Edition*, 214-215.
[32]Castles and Miller, *The Age of Migration*, 112.
[33]*International Migration Outlook: SOPEMI—2008 Edition*, 278.
[34]*International Migration Outlook: SOPEMI—2010 Edition*, 240-241.
[35]Castles and Miller, *The Age of Migration*, 119.
[36]*International Migration Outlook: SOPEMI—2008 Edition*, 242.
[37]Ibid., 243.
[38]*International Migration Outlook: SOPEMI—2010 Edition*, 204.
[39]Rainer Munz, "Migrants, labour markets and integration in Europe: a comparative analysis," *Global Migration Perspectives*, no. 16 (October 2004): 8, http://www.unitar .org.ny/files/GMP_labour%20integration%20Europe.pdf (accessed August 21, 2009).
[40]Castles and Miller, *The Age of Migration*, 119.
[41]*International Migration Outlook: SOPEMI—2008 Edition*, 244.
[42]http://www.oecd.org/dataoecd/39/41/43185270.xls (accessed August 21, 2009).
[43]*International Migration Outlook: SOPEMI—2010 Edition*, 206-207.
[44]*International Migration Outlook: SOPEMI—2008 Edition*, 228-229.
[45]*International Migration Outlook: SOPEMI—2010 Edition*, 190.
[46]*International Migration Outlook: SOPEMI—2008 Edition*, 230-231.
[47]*International Migrant Stock: The 2008 Revision* website.
[48]*International Migration Outlook: SOPEMI—2008 Edition*, 226.
[49]"Perspectives on Migrants, 2009: Permanent Migration to Australia—An Overview by Eligibility Category," Australian Bureau of Statistics website, http://www.abs.gov.au/ AUSSTATS/abs@.nsf/Lookup/3416.0Main+Features22009, (accessed June 12, 2009).
[50]Ibid.
[51]*International Migration Outlook: SOPEMI—2008 Edition*, 227.
[52]Ibid., 226.
[53]*International Migration Outlook: SOPEMI—2010 Edition*, 188.
[54]Australian Department of Immigration and Citizenship, *Immigration Update: 2010-2011* (Department of Immigration and Citizenship, 2011), 14, 15, 16, http://www .immi.gov.au/media/publications/statistics/immigration-update/update-2010-11.pdf (accessed March 27, 2011).

[55]http://www.stats.govt.nz/~/media/Statistics/Census/2001-Census-reports/Snapshot%20 pdfs/2001-census-snapshot14.pdf (accessed August 21, 2009).

[56]*International Migration Outlook: SOPEMI—2008 Edition*, 266.

[57]Statistics New Zealand, "International Travel and Migration: April 2009," *Hot Off the Press*, May 21, 2009, 7, http://media.nzherald.co.nz/webcontent/document/pdf/ internationaltravelandmigrationpdf1.pdf (accessed August 21, 2009).

[58]*International Migration Outlook: SOPEMI—2010 Edition*, 228.

Chapter 3: The World's Unreached in the West

[1]Wendy Stueck, "Highway to Heaven's Many Paths to Salvation," *The Globe and Mail*, December 12, 2010, http://m.theglobeandmail.com/news/national/highway-to-heavens-many-paths-to-salvation/article587274/?service=mobile (accessed June 26, 2012).

[2]A commonly used definition of people group is "the largest group through which the gospel can flow without encountering significant barriers of understanding and acceptance." This definition and number of people groups mentioned in the chapter were taken from the website of the Global Research Department of the International Mission Board. See http://public.imb.org/globalresearch/Pages/default.aspx (accessed January 21, 2011). It should be noted that there is some discrepancy among missiologists regarding the exact number of unreached people groups. For example, Joshua Project lists 16,596 total people groups in the world (as of February 28, 2011). Different numbers usually involve how the peoples are being categorized before being counted. Also, Joshua Project defines an unreached people as having less than 2% evangelicals and 5% or fewer "Christian Adherents" (see www.joshuaproject.net) and, therefore, lists the world's total unreached people groups as 6,870 (as of February 28, 2011).

[3]http://public.imb.org/globalresearch/Pages/default.aspx (accessed January 21, 2011).

[4]http://www.worldchristiandatabase.org/wcd/.

[5]http://www.joshuaproject.net/.

[6]http://www.peoplegroups.org/.

[7]http://www.joshuaproject.net/people-list-comparison-general.php (accessed February 3, 2011).

[8]You can find the data from Joshua Project online at http://www.joshuaproject.net/ and the data from the International Mission Board online at http://www.peoplegroups.org/. While I do not know how frequently Joshua Project updates their data, the International Mission Board updates their data each month.

[9]http://www.joshuaproject.net/definitions.php (accessed February 3, 2011).

[10]http://www.joshuaproject.net/why-include-christian-adherent.php (accessed February 3, 2011).

[11]http://www.peoplegroups.org/faqs.aspx#WhatIsPG (accessed February 3, 2011).

[12]http://www.peoplegroups.org/Detail.aspx?PID=46471 (accessed February 6, 2011).

[13]http://www.grdweb.info/gsec/Overview/tabid/259/Default.aspx (accessed February 6, 2011).

[14]http://www.joshuaproject.net/peoples.php (accessed February 6, 2011).

[15]As of March 28, 2012.

[16]As of March 28, 2012.

[17]Jason Makdryk, *Operation World: The Definitive Prayer Guide to Every Nation*, 7th ed.

(Colorado Springs, CO: Biblica Publishing, 2010), 961. This resource follows closely the people-group listings from Joshua Project.
[18]Global Research data as of March 28, 2012.

Chapter 4: Migration and Kingdom Expansion, Part 1

[1]Patrick Belton, "In the Way of the Prophet: Ideologies and Institutions in Dearborn, Michigan, America's Muslim Capitol," *Next American City* (October 2003), www.patrickbeton.com/dearborn_article.pdf.

Chapter 5: Migration and Kingdom Expansion, Part 2

[1]Joe Friesen and Sandra Martin, "Part 3: Canada's Changing Faith," *The Globe and Mail*, October 5, 2010, http://www.theglobeandmail.com/news/national/time-to-lead/multiculturalism/part-3-canadas-changing-faith/article1741422/ (accessed December 14, 2010.)

[2]James K. Hoffmeier, *The Immigration Crisis: Immigrants, Aliens, and the Bible* (Wheaton, IL: Crossway Books, 2009), 132.

[3]Jehu J. Hanciles, *Beyond Christendom: Globalization, African Migration, and the Transformation of the West* (Maryknoll, NY: Orbis Books, 2008), 140.

Chapter 6: Migration and the West, 1500–2010

[1]Adam Meagher, "Satellite Chinatown," *Next American City*, Summer 2007, http://americancity.org/magazine/article/satellite-chinatown-meagher/ (accessed August 20, 2010).

[2]For an excellent work filled with numerous pictures, maps, and charts, see Russell King, ed., *The History of Human Migration* (London: New Holland Publishers, 2007). See also W. M. Spellman, *The Global Community: Migration and the Making of the Modern World* (Stroud, UK: Sutton Publishing, 2002).

[3]Stephen Castles and Mark J. Miller, *The Age of Migration: International Population Movements in the Modern World*, 4th ed. (New York: The Guilford Press, 2009), 81.

[4]Beverly C. McMillan, ed., *Captive Passage: The Transatlantic Slave Trade and the Making of the Americas* (Old Saybrook, CT: Konecky and Konecky, 2002) 9-10; and King, *History of Human Migration*, 88.

[5]Kerby Miller and Paul Wagner, *Out of Ireland: The Story of Irish Emigration to America* (Washington, DC: Elliott and Clark Publishing, 1994), 10-11.

[6]Castles and Miller, *The Age of Migration*, 84.

[7]Peter Kwong and Dušanka Miščević, *Chinese America: The Untold Story of America's Oldest New Community* (New York and London: The New Press, 2005), x.

[8]Oscar Handlin, *The Uprooted: The Epic Story of the Great Migrations that Made the American People*, 2nd ed. (Boston, MA: Little, Brown and Company, 1979), 32-33.

[9]Castles and Miller, *The Age of Migration*, 84.

[10]Castles and Miller, *The Age of Migration*, 85.

[11]Spellman, *The Global Community*, 74-75.

[12]Castles and Miller, *The Age of Migration*, 86-87.

[13]Jeremy Hein, "France: The Melting Pot of Europe," in *Migration and Immigration: A Global View*, eds. Maura I. Toto Morn and Marixsa Allcea (Westport, CT: Greenwood Press, 2004), 72.

[14]Kwong and Miščević, *Chinese America*, 141, 143.

[15]Toro-Morn and Alicea, *Migration and Immigration*, xix.

[16]Ibid., 67.

[17]http://www.unhcr.org/pages/49c3646cbc.html (accessed February 17, 2011).

[18]http://www.unhcr.org/pages/49da0e466.html (accessed February 17, 2011).

[19]Castles and Miller, *The Age of Migration*.

[20]James Hollifield, "The Emerging Migration State," in *Rethinking Migration: New Theoretical and Empirical Perspectives*, eds. Alejandro Portes and Josh DeWind (New York: Berghahn Books, 2007), 69-70.

[21]Afe Adogame and James V. Spickard, eds., *Religion Crossing Boundaries: Transnational Religious and Social Dynamics in Africa and the New African Diaspora* (Boston: Brill, 2010), 8.

[22]Castles and Miller, *The Age of Migration*, 105-106.

[23]Castles and Miller, *The Age of Migration*, 102.

[24]Laurent Bossard, *The Future of International Migration to OECD Countries: Regional Note West Africa*, OECD, 3, http://www.oecd.org/dataoecd/3/42/43484256.pdf (accessed February 17, 2011).

[25]*International Migrant Stock: The 2008 Revision* website, United Nations Department of Economic and Social Affairs, Population Division, http://esa.un.org/migration/index.asp (accessed February 17, 2011).

Chapter 7: Students on the Move

[1]Martin Baumann, "The Hindu Diaspora in Europe," in *Religious Communities in the Diaspora*, ed. Gerrie ter Haar (Nairobi, Kenya: Acton Publishers, 2001), 104.

[2]"Population in Flux in Immigrant-heavy City Areas," http://yle.fi/uutiset/news/2011/01/population_in_flux_in_immigrant-heavy_city_areas_2307718.html (accessed January 25, 2011).

[3]A. G. Sulzberger and Stacey Solie, "Guatemalans, in Brooklyn for Work, Keep Bonds of Home," *The New York Times*, February 2, 2010, http://www.nytimes.com/2010/02/02/nyregion/02guatemalan.html (accessed February 2, 2010.)

[4]*The New People Next Door: Lausanne Occasional Paper No. 55* (2005), 30, http://www.lausanne.org/documents/2004forum/LOP55_IG26.pdf (accessed January 20, 2011).

[5]UNESCO Institute of Statistics, *Global Education Digest 2010: Comparing Education Statistics Across the World*, 72, http://www.uis.unesco.org/library/documents/GED_2010_EN.pdf (accessed January 20, 2011).

[6]Ibid.

[7]For a list of OECD countries, see http://www.oecd.org/document/58/0,2340,en_2649_201185_1889402_1_1_1_1,00.html (accessed January 20, 2011).

[8]OECD, *International Migration Outlook: SOPEMI—2010 Edition*, 41, http://www.nbbmuseum.be/doc/seminar2010/nl/bibliografie/kansengroepen/sopemi2010.pdf.

[9]Ibid., 41.

[10]Ibid., 45.

[11]Stephen Castles and Mark J. Miller, *The Age of Migration: International Population Movements in the Modern World*, 4th ed. (New York: The Guilford Press, 2009), 141.

[12]*International Migration Outlook: SOPEMI—2010 Edition*, 21.

[13]*Global Education Digest 2010,* 181.

[14]Edward Alden, "U.S. Losing Ground in Competitive Immigration," *World Politics Review* (July 27, 2010): 2.

[15]Institute of International Education, "Open Doors 2011—Fast Facts," http://www.iie.org/en/research-and-publications/~/media/Files/Corporate/Open-Doors/Fast-Facts/Fast%20Facts%202011.ashx (accessed March 27, 2012).

[16]Ibid.

[17]*International Migration Outlook: SOPEMI—2010 Edition,* 196.

[18]"UK rise in international students," BBC News, September 24, 2009, http://news.bbc.co.uk/go/pr/fr/-/2/hi/uk_news/education/8271287.stm

[19]*International Migration Outlook: SOPEMI—2010 Edition,* 190.

[20]OECD, International Migration Outlook: SOPEMI—2008 Edition, 3, http://www.oecd.org/dataoecd/30/13/41275373.pdf (accessed February 28, 2011).

[21]*International Migration Outlook: SOPEMI—2010 Edition,* 204.

[22]Ibid., 202.

[23]Ibid., 200.

[24]Ibid., 242.

[25]Ibid., 207, 215, 227, 230, 235, 241, 245.

[26]Ibid., 228.

[27]*International Migration Outlook: SOPEMI—2008 Edition,* 3.

[28]http://www.uis.unesco.org/library/documents/GED_2010_EN.pdf.

[29]Australian Bureau of Statistics, *Year Book Australia 2009-2010,* http://www.abs.gov.au/AUSSTATS/abs@.nsf/Lookup/609E05EF5CAE0061CA25773700169C94?opendocument (accessed January 21, 2011).

[30]Australian Government, Department of Immigration and Citizenship, *Immigration Update 2010-2011,* 38, http://www.immi.gov.au/media/publications/statistics/immigration-update/update-2010-11.pdf (accessed March 27, 2012).

[31]*New People Next Door,* 28.

[32]Brooklyn Lowery, "Louisiana Churches Reach Out to International Students," *Facts and Trends* 56, no.4 (Fall 2010): 9.

[33]Carol Pipes, "Former Muslim shares Gospel amid Toronto's ethnic diversity," Baptist Press, February 9, 2010, http://www.bpnews.net/bpnews.asp?id=32254 (accessed January 20, 2011).

[34]Tom Phillips and Bob Norsworthy, with W. Terry Whalin, *The World at Your Door: Reaching International Students in Your Home, Church, and School* (Minneapolis, MN: Bethany House Publishers, 1997), 32.

Chapter 8: Refugees on the Move

[1]Martin Baumann, "The Hindu Diaspora in Europe," in *Religious Communities in the Diaspora,* ed. Gerrie ter Haar (Nairobi, Kenya: Acton Publishers, 2001), 89, 100.

[2]Nathal Dessing, "Circumcision of Muslim Boys in the Netherlands," in *Religious Communities in the Diaspora,* ed. Gerrie ter Haar (Nairobi, Kenya: Acton Publishers, 2001), 130.

[3]"First of 60,000 refugees from Bhutan arrive in U.S.," CNN World, March 25, 2008, http://articles.cnn.com/2008-03-25/world/bhutan.refugees_1_bhutan-resettlement-plan-refugees-claim?_s=PM (accessed June 21, 2010).

[4]Mya Frazier, "Somalia on the Scioto: What immigrants mean for the future of Columbus," *Next American City,* Summer 2010, 48-53, http://americancity.org/magazine/article/somalia-on-the-scioto/ (accessed October 3, 2011).

[5]Ted C. Lewellen, *The Anthropology of Globalization: Cultural Anthropology Enters the 21st Century* (Westport, CT: Bergin and Garvey, 2002), 174.

[6]http://www.unhcr.org/pages/49c3646cbc.html (accessed January 23, 2011).

[7]UNHCR, *Convention and Protocol Relating to the Status of Refugees,* 16, http://www.unhcr.org/3b66c2aa10.html (accessed January 23, 2011).

[8]For the definition of an asylum seeker, see chapter 1.

[9]"UNHCR Statistical Yearbook 2010," 6, 7, 8, 9, 21, 25, http://www.unhcr.org/4ef9cc9c9.html (accessed March 27, 2012).

[10]Ibid., 6.

[11]"UNHCR Statistical Yearbook 2010," Annex, http://www.unhcr.org/4ef9c7269.html (accessed March 27, 2012).

[12]Ibid., 13.

[13]Ibid., 17.

[14]UNHCR, *Asylum Levels and Trends in Industralized Countries, 2009: Statistical Overview of Asylum Applications Lodged in Europe and Selected Non-European Countries,* 5-7, http://www.unhcr.org/4ba7341a9.html (accessed January 24, 2011). This study was based on the thirty-eight European and six non-European countries that currently provide monthly asylum statistics to UNHCR.

[15]Alan Travis, "Figures show 20% increase in net migration to UK," *Guardian,* August 26, 2010, http://www.guardian.co.uk/uk/2010/aug/26/net-migration-to-uk-increases (accessed August 31, 2010).

[16]"UNHCR Statistical Yearbook 2010," Annex, 62, 63, 64, http://www.unhcr.org/4ef9c7269.html (accessed March 27, 2012).

[17]*2009 Global Trends,* 12 (accessed January 23, 2011).

[18]Ibid., 18.

[19]*Asylum Levels and Trends,* 10-11.

[20]Will Somerville, Dhananjayan Sriskandarajah, and Maria Latorre, "United Kingdom: A Reluctant Country of Immigration," *Migration Information Source,* July 2009, http://www.migrationinformation.org/feature/display.cfm?ID=736 (accessed January 24, 2011).

[21]Daniel C. Martin, "Refugees and Asylees: 2010," May 2011, 3, U.S. Department of Homeland Security, http://www.dhs.gov/xlibrary/assets/statistics/publications/ois_rfa_fr_2010.pdf (accessed March 27, 2012).

[22]*2009 Global Trends,* 10-11.

[23]Kristen Chick, "Libya crisis: neighbors brace as tide of refugees rises," *Christian Science Monitor,* February 28, 2011, http://www.csmonitor.com/World/Middle-East/2011/0228/Libya-crisis-neighbors-brace-as-tide-of-refugees-rises (accessed February 28, 2011).

Chapter 9: Stories from the Field
[1]Statistics New Zealand, *Demographic Trends: 2007,* 110, http://www.stats.govt.nz/browse_for_stats/population/estimates_and_projections/demographic-trends-2007.aspx (accessed January 25, 2011).

[2]BBC News, "Germany's Turks Urged to Learn German to Integrate," October 19, 2010,

http://www.bbc.co.uk/news/world-europe-11578657 (accessed October 20, 2010).

[3]Martin Baumann, "The Hindu Diaspora in Europe," in *Religious Communities in the Diaspora,* ed. Gerrie ter Haar (Nairobi, Kenya: Acton Publishers, 2001), 103, 105.

[4]Laurent Bossard, "The Future of International Migration to OECD Countries Regional Note West Africa," OECD, http://www.oecd.org/dataoecd/3/42/43484256.pdf (accessed January 25, 2011).

[5]David Boyd, *You Don't Have to Cross the Ocean to Reach the World* (Grand Rapids, MI: Chosen Books, 2008), 148-149.

[6]Ibid., 184.

[7]Myunghee Lee, "Migrant Workers' Churches as Welcoming, Sending and Recruiting Entities: A Case Study of Mongolian Migrant Workers' Churches in Korea" in *Missions from the Majority World: Progress, Challenges, and Case Studies,* eds. Enoch Wan and Michael Pocock (Pasadena, CA: William Carey Library, 2009), 377-378.

[8]Ibid., 379.

[9]Ibid.

[10]Minho Song, "The Diaspora Experience of the Korean Church and Its Implications for World Missions," in *Korean Diaspora and Christian Missions,* eds. S. Hun Kim and Wonsuk Ma (Eugene, OR: Wipf and Stock Publishers, 2011), 109.

[11]Jared Looney, "Transcending Borders: Cities as Nodes for Transnational Evangelism," *Journal of Urban Mission* 1, no. 3 (November 2, 2010), http://jofum.com/editorial/articles/transcending-borders-cities-as-nodes-for-transnational-evangelism/ (accessed November 4, 2010).

[12]Sharon Mager, "Five hundred come to Christ and two churches start as a result of Nepal/India mission trip" *Baptist Life,* August 2009, http://www.baptistlifeonline.org/2009/08/five-hundred-come-to-christ-and-two-churches-start-as-a-result-of-nepalindia-mission-trip/ (accessed February 7, 2011).

[13]Looney, "Transcending Borders."

Chapter 10: Guidelines for Reaching the Strangers Next Door

[1]Australian Bureau of Statistics, *Year Book Australia,* 2009-10, April 6, 2010: 618-20, http://www.abs.gov.au/ausstats/abs@.nsf/mf/1301.0 (accessed January 3, 2011).

[2]Statistics New Zealand, *Demographic Trends: 2007,* 110, http://www.stats.govt.nz/browse_for_stats/population/estimates_and_projections/demographic-trends-2007.aspx (accessed January 25, 2011).

[3]Donald McGavran, *The Bridges of God: A Study in the Strategy of Missions* (Eugene, OR: Wipf and Stock Publishers, 2005).

[4]Terrence Lyons and Peter Mandaville, "Diasporas Shape Politics Back Home from Afar," *YaleGlobal Online,* November 19, 2010, http://yaleglobal.yale.edu/content/diasporas-shape-politics-back-home (accessed November 23, 2010).

[5]International Organization for Migration, *Migration and Religion in a Globalized World,* 30, December 2005, http://iom.int/jahia/webdav/shared/shared/mainsite/published_docs/books/Migration%20and%20Religion-new_LR.pdf (accessed February 11, 2011).

[6]Timothy Paul, "Impacting the Hindu Diaspora in North America," *International Journal of Frontier Missiology* 26, no. 3 (Fall 2009): 130.

[7]Ibid.

[8]Enoch Wan, "Mission among the Chinese Diaspora: A Case Study of Migration and Mission," *Missiology* 31, no.1 (January 2003): 36.

[9]Sharon A. Suh, "Buddhism, Rhetoric, and the Korean American Community," in *Immigration and Religion in America: Comparative and Historical Perspectives,* eds. Richard Alba, Albert J. Raboteau, and Josh DeWind (New York: New York University Press, 2008), 166.

[10]Jehu J. Hanciles, *Beyond Christendom: Globalization, African Migration, and the Transformation of the West* (Maryknoll, NY: Orbis Books, 2008), 297.

[11]John Beya, "Francophone Presence in Britain," in *Religious Communities in the Diaspora,* ed. Gerrie ter Haar (Nairobi, Kenya: Acton Publishers, 2001), 214-215.

[12]The ranking was completed on a five-point Likert scale. The more receptive had an average score above 3.9, while the less receptive had an average score below 3.0. See Brooklyn Lowery, "LifeWay Research Finds Outreach to First-Generation Immigrants Succeeding, Needs Improvement" (March 29, 2010), http://www.lifeway.com/article/170199/. The PowerPoint presentation of the research, titled "NAMB First Generation Immigration Results from National Leaders," can be found at http://www.faithformationlearning exchange.net/uploads/5/2/4/6/5246709/first_generation_immigrant_research_presen tation_-_lifeway_research.ppt (accessed June 26, 2012).

[13]*Migration and Religion in a Globalized World,* 32-33.

[14]Donna S. Thomas, *Faces in the Crowd: Reaching Your International Neighbor for Christ* (Birmingham, AL: New Hope Publishers, 2008), 141.

[15]I explain this matter and other church-planting issues in detail in my book *Discovering Church Planting: An Introduction to the Hows, Whats, and Whys of Global Church Planting* (Colorado Springs, CO: Paternoster, 2009).

[16]Charles Brock, *Indigenous Church Planting: A Practical Journey* (Neosho, MO: Church Growth International, 1994), 130.

Chapter 11: A Suggested Strategy for Reaching the Strangers Next Door

[1]"Study: Canada's visible minority population in 2017," *The Daily,* March 22, 2005, www.statcan.gc.ca/daily-quotidien/050322/dq050322b-eng.htm.

[2]For a more detailed treatment on developing missionary strategy, I direct you to the forthcoming book by John Mark Terry and me: *Strategy Matters: Missionary Strategy and Global Disciple Making* [tentative title] (Grand Rapids, MI: Baker Academic, forthcoming).

[3]"Tunisia refugees flood Italian island," Aljazeera, February 14, 2011, http://aljazeera .com/video/africa/2011/02/201121463028172925.html (accessed February 14, 2011) and BBC documentary, "The Chinese Are Coming," www.bbc.co.uk/programmes/ b00ykxg9.

[4]Brooklyn Lowery, "Louisiana Churches Reach Out to International Students," *Facts and Trends* 56, no. 4 (Fall 2010): 8, http://www.lifeway.com/article/170615/ (accessed February 14, 2011).

[5]Dale Martin, "Radicalization or Assimilation? Diaspora Muslims in Europe and North America," *Seedbed* 24, no. 1 (August 2010): 56.

[6]David Chul Han Jun, "A South Korean Case Study of Migrant Ministries," in *Korean Diaspora and Christian Mission,* eds. S. Hun Kim and Wonsuk Ma (Eugene, OR: Wipf and Stock Publishers, 2011), 221.

[7]Gerrie ter Haar, "The African Diaspora in Europe: Some Important Themes and Issues," in *Strangers and Sojourners: Religious Communities in the Diaspora,* ed. Gerrie ter Haar (Leuven, Belgium: Peeters, 1998), 49.

Chapter 12: Diaspora Missiology

[1]Samuel Escobar, *The New Global Mission: The Gospel from Everywhere to Everywhere* (Downers Grove, IL: InterVarsity Press, 2003), 11.

[2]You can obtain a PDF download of *Scattered to Gather: Embracing the Global Trend of Diaspora* (Manila, Philippines: LifeChange Publishing, 2010) at http://www.jdpayne .org/wp-content/uploads/2010/10/Scattered-to-Gather.pdf. Also, I have several posts on my blog related to diaspora missiology, including interviews with Dr. Sadiri Joy Tira and videos from Lausanne III in Cape Town. You can find them at http://www.jdpayne .org/2010/10/20/interview-with-dr-sadiri-joy-tira-from-cape-town-2010/ (accessed February 13, 2011). Enoch Wan has written an excellent article addressing diaspora missiology, beginning on the third page of the *Occasional Bulletin* (Spring 2007). It can be found at http://www.emsweb.org/images/stories/docs/bulletins/OB_20_2.pdf.

While there are a growing number of resources being written on diaspora missiology, the following are a few excellent books to get you started in understanding this field: Enoch Wan, ed., *Missions within Reach: Intercultural Ministries in Canada* (Edmonton, Alberta, Canada: China Alliance Press, 1995); Luis Pantoja, Jr., Sadiri Joy Tira, Enoch Wan, eds., *Scattered: The Filipino Global Presence* (Manila, Philippines: LifeChange Publishing Inc., 2004); Enoch Wan and Sadiri Joy Tira, eds., *Missions Practice in the 21st Century* (Pasadena, CA: William Carey International University Press, 2009); Jehu J. Hanciles, *Beyond Christendom: Globalization, African Migration, and the Transformation of the West* (Maryknoll, NY: Orbis Books, 2008); Enoch Wan and Michael Pocock, eds., *Missions from the Majority World: Progress, Challenges, and Case Studies* (Pasadena, CA: William Carey Library, 2009); Thorsten Prill, *Global Mission on Our Doorstep: Forced Migration and the Future of the Church* (Münster, Germany: MV Wissenschaft, 2008); S. Hun Kim and Wonsuk Ma, eds., *Korean Diaspora and Christian Mission* (Eugene, OR: Wipf and Stock Publishers, 2011); Sadiri Emmanuel Santiago B. Tira, *Filipino Kingdom Workers: An Ethnographic Study in Diaspora Missiology* (Pasadena, CA: William Carey International University Press, 2012); and Enoch Wan, ed., *Diaspora Missiology: Theory, Methodology, and Practice* (n.p.: CreateSpace, 2012), Sadiri Joy Tira, ed., *The Human Tidal Wave* (n.p.: LifeChange Publishing, forthcoming).

[3]Enoch Wan, "The Phenomenon of Diaspora: Missiological Implications for Christian Missions," in *Scattered: The Filipino Global Presence,* eds. Luis Pantoja, Jr., Sadiri Joy Tira, and Enoch Wan (Manila, Philippines: LifeChange Publishing, 2004), 110.

[4]*Scattered to Gather,* 27.

[5]Lynellyn D. Long and Ellen Oxfeld, eds., *Coming Home: Refugees, Migrants, and Those Who Stayed Behind* (Philadelphia: University of Pennsylvania Press, 2004), 1-2.

[6]Maxine Margolis, "Transnationalism and Popular Culture: The Case of Brazilian Immigrants in the United States," *Journal of Popular Culture* 29 (1995): 31.

[7]Scattered to Gather, 28.

[8]Claudia Währisch-Oblau, "From Reverse Mission to Common Mission . . . We Hope," *International Review of Mission* 89, no. 354: 470.

[9]Jason Mandryk, *Operation World: The Definitive Prayer Guide to Every Nation*, 7th ed., (Colorado Springs, CO: Biblica Publishing, 2010), 949.

[10]Ibid., 951. According to Mandryk, these statistics are limited to Protestant, independent, and Anglican missionaries serving longer than two years, "but are not limited to international or cross-cultural workers" (p. 950). The table above reflects a revision to the data found in *Operation World* (7th edition). In an email to me (March 30, 2012), Jason Mandryk shared that he is now using the figure of 20,000 for China, PRC, (down from 100,000) due to "a differing understanding of some of the definitions and conditions." Jason requested that I make this change in this table to better reflect the most up-to-date research.

[11]Jehu J. Hanciles, *Beyond Christendom: Globalization, African Migration, and the Transformation of the West* (Maryknoll, NY: Orbis Books, 2008), 6. (Emphasis in the original.)

[12]Jan A. B. Jongeneel, "The Mission of Migrant Churches in Europe," *Missiology* 31, no. 1 (January 2003): 30.

[13]David Lundy, "Multiculturalism and Pluralization: Kissing Cousins of Globalization," in *One World or Many? The Impact of Globalisation on Mission,* ed. Richard Tiplady (Pasadena, CA: William Carey Library, 2003), 73.

[14]Hanciles, *Beyond Christendom,* 298.

[15]Gerrie ter Haar, "African Christians in the Netherlands," in *Religious Communities in the Diaspora,* ed. Gerrie ter Haar (Nairobi, Kenya: Acton Publishers, 2001), 166.

[16]Winston Smith, "Bridge Peoples: The Role of Ethnic Minorities in Global Evangelization," *Lausanne World Pulse,* May 2010, http://www.lausanneworldpulse.com/themedarticles.php/1275/05-2010 (accessed June 4, 2010).

Scripture Index